Salty Kisses

A Sanderling Cove Inn Book - 3

Judith Keim

Wild Quail Publishing

BOOKS BY JUDITH KEIM

THE HARTWELL WOMEN SERIES:

The Talking Tree – 1
Sweet Talk – 2
Straight Talk – 3
Baby Talk – 4
The Hartwell Women – Boxed Set

THE BEACH HOUSE HOTEL SERIES:

Breakfast at The Beach House Hotel – 1
Lunch at The Beach House Hotel – 2
Dinner at The Beach House Hotel – 3
Christmas at The Beach House Hotel – 4
Margaritas at The Beach House Hotel – 5
Dessert at The Beach House Hotel – 6
Coffee at The Beach House Hotel – 7 (2023)
High Tea at The Beach House hotel – 8 (2024)

THE FAT FRIDAYS GROUP:

Fat Fridays – 1
Sassy Saturdays – 2
Secret Sundays – 3

THE SALTY KEY INN SERIES:

Finding Me – 1
Finding My Way – 2
Finding Love – 3
Finding Family – 4
The Salty Key Inn Series . Boxed Set

THE CHANDLER HILL INN SERIES:

Going Home – 1
Coming Home – 2
Home at Last – 3
The Chandler Hill Inn Series – Boxed Set

SEASHELL COTTAGE BOOKS:

A Christmas Star
Change of Heart
A Summer of Surprises
A Road Trip to Remember
The Beach Babes

THE DESERT SAGE INN SERIES:

The Desert Flowers – Rose – 1
The Desert Flowers – Lily – 2
The Desert Flowers – Willow – 3
The Desert Flowers – Mistletoe and Holly – 4

SOUL SISTERS AT CEDAR MOUNTAIN LODGE:

Christmas Sisters – Anthology
Christmas Kisses
Christmas Castles
Christmas Stories – Soul Sisters Anthology
Christmas Joy
The Christmas Joy Boxed Set

THE SANDERLING COVE INN SERIES:

Waves of Hope – 1
Sandy Wishes – 2
Salty Kisses – 3

THE LILAC LAKE INN SERIES

Love by Design – (2023)
Love Between the Lines – (2023)
Love Under the Stars – (2024)

OTHER BOOKS:

The ABC's of Living With a Dachshund
Once Upon a Friendship – Anthology

Winning BIG – a little love story for all ages
Holiday Hopes
The Winning Tickets (2023)

For more information: **www.judithkeim.com**

PRAISE FOR JUDITH KEIM'S NOVELS

THE BEACH HOUSE HOTEL SERIES

"Love the characters in this series. This series was my first introduction to Judith Keim. She is now one of my favorites. Looking forward to reading more of her books."

BREAKFAST AT THE BEACH HOUSE HOTEL is an easy, delightful read that offers romance, family relationships, and strong women learning to be stronger. Real life situations filter through the pages. Enjoy!"

LUNCH AT THE BEACH HOUSE HOTEL – "This series is such a joy to read. You feel you are actually living with them. Can't wait to read the latest one."

DINNER AT THE BEACH HOUSE HOTEL – "A Terrific Read! As usual, Judith Keim did it again. Enjoyed immensely. Continue writing such pleasantly reading books for all of us readers."

CHRISTMAS AT THE BEACH HOUSE HOTEL – "Not Just Another Christmas Novel. This is book number four in the series and my introduction to Judith Keim's writing. I wasn't disappointed. The characters are dimensional and engaging. The plot is well crafted and advances at a pleasing pace. The Florida location is interesting and warming. It was a delight to read a romance novel with mature female protagonists. Ann and Rhoda have life experiences that enrich the story. It's a clever book about friends and extended family. Buy copies for your book group pals and enjoy this seasonal read."

MARGARITAS AT THE BEACH HOUSE HOTEL – "What a wonderful series. I absolutely loved this book and can't wait for the next book to come out. There was even suspense in it. Thanks Judith for the great stories."

"Overall, Margaritas at the Beach House Hotel is another wonderful addition to the series. Judith Keim takes the reader on a journey told through the voices of these amazing characters we have all come to love through the years! I truly cannot stress enough how good this book is, and I hope you enjoy it as much as I have!"

THE HARTWELL WOMEN SERIES:

"This was an EXCELLENT series. When I discovered Judith Keim, I read all of her books back to back. I thoroughly enjoyed the women Keim has written about. They are believable and you want to just jump into their lives and be their friends! I can't wait for any upcoming books!"

"I fell into Judith Keim's Hartwell Women series and have read & enjoyed all of her books in every series. Each centers around a strong & interesting woman character and their family interaction. Good reads that leave you wanting more."

THE FAT FRIDAYS GROUP :

"Excellent story line for each character, and an insightful representation of situations which deal with some of the contemporary issues women are faced with today."

"I love this author's books. Her characters and their lives are realistic. The power of women's friendships is a common and beautiful theme that is threaded throughout this story."

THE SALTY KEY INN SERIES

<u>FINDING ME</u> – "I thoroughly enjoyed the first book in this series and cannot wait for the others! The characters are endearing with the same struggles we all encounter. The setting makes me feel like I am a guest at The Salty Key

Inn...relaxed, happy & light-hearted! The men are yummy and the women strong. You can't get better than that! Happy Reading!"

FINDING MY WAY- *"Loved the family dynamics as well as uncertain emotions of dating and falling in love. Appreciated the morals and strength of parenting throughout. Just couldn't put this book down."*

FINDING LOVE – *"I waited for this book because the first two was such good reads. This one didn't disappoint.... Judith Keim always puts substance into her books. This book was no different, I learned about PTSD, accepting oneself, there is always going to be problems but stick it out and make it work. Just the way life is. In some ways a lot like my life. Judith is right, it needs another book and I will definitely be reading it. Hope you choose to read this series, you will get so much out of it."*

FINDING FAMILY – *"Completing this series is like eating the last chip. Love Judith's writing, and her female characters are always smart, strong, vulnerable to life and love experiences."*

"This was a refreshing book. Bringing the heart and soul of the family to us."

THE CHANDLER HILL INN SERIES

GOING HOME – *"I absolutely could not put this book down. Started at night and read late into the middle of the night. As a child of the '60s, the Vietnam war was front and center so this resonated with me. All the characters in the book were so well developed that the reader felt like they were friends of the family."*

"I was completely immersed in this book, with the beautiful descriptive writing, and the authors' way of

bringing her characters to life. I felt like I was right inside her story."

COMING HOME – "Coming Home is a winner. The characters are well-developed, nuanced and likable. Enjoyed the vineyard setting, learning about wine growing and seeing the challenges Cami faces in running and growing a business. I look forward to the next book in this series!"

"Coming Home was such a wonderful story. The author has a gift for getting the reader right to the heart of things."

HOME AT LAST – "In this wonderful conclusion, to a heartfelt and emotional trilogy set in Oregon's stunning wine country, Judith Keim has tied up the Chandler Hill series with the perfect bow."

"Overall, this is truly a wonderful addition to the Chandler Hill Inn series. Judith Keim definitely knows how to perfectly weave together a beautiful and heartfelt story."

"The storyline has some beautiful scenes along with family drama. Judith Keim has created characters with interactions that are believable and some of the subjects the story deals with are poignant."

SEASHELL COTTAGE BOOKS

A CHRISTMAS STAR – "Love, laughter, sadness, great food, and hope for the future, all in one book. It doesn't get any better than this stunning read."

"A Christmas Star is a heartwarming Christmas story featuring endearing characters. So many Christmas books are set in snowbound places...it was a nice change to read a Christmas story that takes place on a warm sandy beach!" Susan Peterson

CHANGE OF HEART – "CHANGE OF HEART is the

summer read we've all been waiting for. Judith Keim is a master at creating fascinating characters that are simply irresistible. Her stories leave you with a big smile on your face and a heart bursting with love."

Kellie Coates Gilbert, author of the popular Sun Valley Series

A SUMMER OF SURPRISES – "The story is filled with a roller coaster of emotions and self-discovery. Finding love again and rebuilding family relationships."

"Ms. Keim uses this book as an amazing platform to show that with hard emotional work, belief in yourself and love, the scars of abuse can be conquered. It in no way preaches, it's a lovely story with a happy ending."

"The character development was excellent. I felt I knew these people my whole life. The story development was very well thought out I was drawn [in] from the beginning."

THE DESERT SAGE INN SERIES:

THE DESERT FLOWERS – ROSE – "The Desert Flowers - Rose, is the first book in the new series by Judith Keim. I always look forward to new books by Judith Keim, and this one is definitely a wonderful way to begin The Desert Sage Inn Series!"

"In this first of a series, we see each woman come into her own and view new beginnings even as they must take this tearful journey as they slowly lose a dear friend. This is a very well written book with well-developed and likable main characters. It was interesting and enlightening as the first portion of this saga unfolded. I very much enjoyed this book and I do recommend it"

"Judith Keim is one of those authors that you can always depend on to give you a great story with fantastic characters. I'm excited to know that she is writing a new

series and after reading book 1 in the series, I can't wait to read the rest of the books."!

<u>*THE DESERT FLOWERS – LILY*</u> – *"The second book in the Desert Flowers series is just as wonderful as the first. Judith Keim is a brilliant storyteller. Her characters are truly lovely and people that you want to be friends with as soon as you start reading. Judith Keim is not afraid to weave real life conflict and loss into her stories. I loved reading Lily's story and can't wait for Willow's!*

"The Desert Flowers-Lily is the second book in The Desert Sage Inn Series by author Judith Keim. When I read the first book in the series, The Desert Flowers-Rose, I knew this series would exceed all of my expectations and then some. Judith Keim is an amazing author, and this series is a testament to her writing skills and her ability to completely draw a reader into the world of her characters."

<u>*THE DESERT FLOWERS – WILLOW –*</u> *"The feelings of love, joy, happiness, friendship, family and the pain of loss are deeply felt by Willow Sanchez and her two cohorts Rose and Lily. The Desert Flowers met because of their deep feelings for Alec Thurston, a man who touched their lives in different ways.*

Once again, Judith Keim has written the story of a strong, competent, confident and independent woman. Willow, like Rose and Lily can handle tough situations. All the characters are written so that the reader gets to know them but not all the characters will give the reader warm and fuzzy feelings.

The story is well written and from the start you will be pulled in. There is enough backstory that a reader can start here but I assure you, you'll want to learn more. There is an ocean of emotions that will make you smile, cringe, tear up or outright cry. I loved this book as I loved books one and two. I am thrilled that the Desert Flowers story will continue. I highly recommend this book to anyone who enjoys books with strong women."

Salty Kisses

A Sanderling Cove Inn Book - 3

Judith Keim

Wild Quail Publishing

wildquail.pub@gmail.com

www.judithkeim.com

Published in the United States of America by:

Wild Quail Publishing
PO Box 171332
Boise, ID 83717-1332

ISBN# 978-1-962452-09-0

Dedication

This book is dedicated to those people who discover the joy of art in all its many forms and share it with others.

The Five Families of Sanderling Cove

Gran – **Eleanor "Ellie" Weatherby** – dating John Rizzo – husband deceased – 3 daughters:

Vanessa m. Walter Van Pelt, JoAnn single, Leigh m. Jake Winters

Granddaughter – ***Charlotte "Charlie" Bradford*** (Vanessa's daughter)

Granddaughter – ***Brooke Weatherby*** (Jo's daughter)

Granddaughter – ***Olivia "Livy" Winters*** (Leigh's daughter)

Granny Liz – **Elizabeth "Liz" Ensley** – husband Sam - 2 sons:

Henry, m. Diana, divorced, then m. Savannah, and 1 son never married

Grandson – ***Shane Ensley***– lawyer in Miami

Grandson – ***Austin Ensley***– IT guru who sold business and is looking for next opportunity

***Mimi*-** **Karen Atkins** – husband deceased – 1 son, Arthur Atkins, and 1 daughter:

KK. m. Gordon Hendrix,

Grandson -***Dylan Hendrix*** – artist

Granddaughter -***Grace Hendrix*** m. Belinda – owns restaurant called Gills in Clearwater

Arthur m. Elizabeth Brownley

Grandson – ***Adam Atkins*** m. Summer, divorced has daughter Skye

Grandson – ***Brendan Atkins*** – in construction business with Adam

G-Ma **– Sarah Simon** – husband Joel deceased - 1 son: Benjamin:

Grandson – ***Eric Simon***- plastic surgeon in Tampa, specializes in cleft palates

Granddaughter – ***Shelby Simon*** m. Douglas Sheehan baby due

Grandma **– Pat Dunlap** – husband Ed – 1 daughter:

Katherine m. William Worthington

Grandson – ***Kyle Worthington*** - talent agent in Hollywood

Granddaughter – ***Melissa Worthington***– engaged to Texas oilman

Granddaughter – ***Morgan Worthington***– spoiled baby of family

CHAPTER ONE

ELLIE

From her table on the plaza in a small town in Greece, Ellie Weatherby Rizzo looked out at the activity and sighed with pleasure. She and her husband, John, were fortunate to have this time to travel through Europe after working at The Sanderling Cove Inn on the Gulf Coast of Florida for years. They couldn't have taken this vacation without the help of their three granddaughters, Charlotte, Brooke, and Olivia, who were running the Inn together while Ellie and John were away.

Ellie cherished the memory of their granddaughters' excitement at the opportunity to leave their old lives behind in order to accept her request for help. Little did they know that she and the four other grandmothers who lived at the cove had other plans in mind. Tired of seeing their beloved grandchildren's lives unsettled, they'd decided to bring all the cove kids together. What better way for their grandbabies to find suitable mates?

Charlotte and Brooke had already become engaged this summer—Charlotte to Liz's grandson Shane, and Brooke to Karen's grandson, Dylan. That left Livy still uncommitted.

Ellie had someone in mind for her, but planning can do only so much. Time would take care of the rest, she hoped. And then she and John could return to Florida and their Inn. Whether the Inn would stay in the family was another decision yet to be made.

"Ellie, you have a devilish smile on your face," said John. "What scheme are you cooking up now?"

Her smile grew broader. “I was thinking how much I love you and our family.”

He reached across the table and took hold of her hand. “Not as much as we love you.”

She sighed happily. She and John were in their seventies, but age didn’t matter when it came to love. This trip would be truly successful if Livy could find the man of her dreams.

CHAPTER TWO

LIVY

Olivia "Livy" Winters walked the shoreline of Sanderling Cove with troubled steps. Since coming to the cove to help her two cousins run their grandparents' Inn, she'd tried to ignore her feelings, but different thoughts kept popping up in her mind like circling sharks about to attack. She couldn't continue. She had to find someone she could trust to help her. Her cousins, Charlotte and Brooke, would gladly support her, but she wasn't ready to share this with them. Not yet. They were happily engaged and thinking of bright futures with their fiancés. Livy didn't want to take any of that excitement away from this special time for them.

She looked down at her feet standing in the lacy foam of the Gulf water as one wave and then another reached her with salty kisses. Their soothing rhythm helped settle the turmoil roiling within her. Seagulls and terns whirled in the sky above her, their cries beckoning people to join them on this early August morning. In a few more weeks, Gran and John would return, and Livy would have to make some important decisions—career, housing, life.

Livy kicked at the water sending spray into the air, creating drops of water that resembled diamonds flying up to the sun. Nearby, the fronds of palm trees whispered in the wind as if they too had a secret to tell.

Following the trail of tiny footprints left behind by sandpipers, sanderlings, and other shore birds, Livy was startled when someone called her name. She turned to see

Skye, Adam Atkins' four-year-old daughter running to her. Adam was Mimi's divorced grandson who was temporarily living with her at the cove.

Livy opened her arms, waited, and then swept Skye to her. She adored this sweet little girl who was curious about the world around her. "Hey, Skye. Are you looking for more shells today?"

Skye's blue eyes shone beneath the pink sun bonnet she wore. "I'm looking for pink shells. Mimi and I are making a wedding picture for Gran and Mr. John."

"A wedding picture? How lovely," said Livy, giving Skye another squeeze before setting her down and glancing at Adam walking their way.

"Hi, Livy. Not working the kitchen at the Inn today?" said Adam when he reached them.

"Not until later. Most of the breakfast group was off to an early start so I could squeeze out some time for myself. I'm trying to do it more and more."

"We all need to do that," said Adam with a note of sadness to his voice.

They stood a moment and watched while Skye ran to catch a wave. "I'm sorry about what happened with your ex," Livy said to him. "I know you were hoping for Skye's sake that she'd changed."

"Thanks. That is the end of my trying to make any relationship work. I don't trust her anymore. Skye's happier when her mother isn't around. Moving forward, we'll just let nature take its course."

"A smart idea," Livy said. She liked Adam. A big affable man, he'd been a natural leader in the sports games the cove kids had played when they all were growing up. Now, after moving back to Florida, he'd bought an older house to fix-up while he started a new job as a supervisor with a local, well-respected construction company. This kept him busy as he began to set up his own business. His grandmother, Mimi, was delighted with his move and temporarily adding two people to her household.

"Happy shell hunting," Livy said. "I'm headed down the beach. See you later." It was such a relief to give herself permission to do her own thing. In the past, she'd ask if Skye needed help or continue talking to Adam out of politeness. She wasn't being rude, just allowing herself to make choices based on what she wanted.

As she continued walking, she considered her past. She'd had a pleasant childhood, but it had sometimes been marred by the competition between her and SueEllen Sutton, the girl next door. It was hard when your mother constantly compared you to someone else, and you came out lacking. The more her mother wanted her to be like SueEllen, embracing a southern feminine role, the more Livy fought against it. She could've married early like SueEllen—she'd had more than one man who wanted a serious relationship. But she never felt ready.

After graduating from culinary school, all she'd wanted was to run her own successful business. Too bad her business partner had been willing to throw away her dream and replace it with the goals her "boyfriend" was chasing.

Livy stopped walking and faced the water. Dating Wayne Chesterton had been the biggest mistake of all. A shiver raced through her. She didn't know if she'd ever get over what he'd put her through. She felt the sting of tears and couldn't prevent them from rolling down her cheeks. She needed to let it go. But how?

Moments later, she brought out a tissue from the pocket of her shorts and wiped her eyes, thankful no one was around.

As she headed back to the Inn, she heard footsteps

pounding on the sand behind her and turned to see Austin Ensley jogging toward her. A smile spread across her face. He'd been her crush when she was a teenager, and though she tried to keep anyone from knowing, she still was attracted to him.

"Hey, Livy, just the person I want to see," he said, stopping beside her. He removed the white towel wrapped around his neck to wipe his face. His dimple appeared as he smiled at her. "I've been trying to set up a time to take you out to dinner as a thank you for standing by me throughout the memorial service for my mother. Knowing I could count on you helped me get through that difficult time. I really want to do this. How about this evening? I talked to Brooke and Charlie, and they said you don't have duties at the Inn tonight."

Realizing any attempt to sidestep the invitation would be rude, Livy did her best to smile. Being with him always made her nervous. She looked at his ripped body, his sandy-colored hair, and the way his blue-eyed gaze had settled on her and took a deep breath.

"Well?" he asked.

"That would be nice, Austin, but you know my intention was to support you, nothing more."

"And you did," he said. "Where would you like to go? We could try Gavin's at the Salty Key Inn, the Don Cesar Hotel, or any fancy place you want." He made it difficult to say no.

"How about we keep it simple?" Livy said. "How about The Crab Shack?"

His lips curved. "Should be fun. I'll pick you up at six thirty, if that's okay."

"Sure. Thanks, Austin." The melancholy that had gripped her earlier faded. Austin was an interesting man, and conversation would keep the evening going. She started to walk away.

He came up beside her and casually swung an arm around her shoulder. "Are you all right?"

She looked up at him in surprise.

He thumbed a tear from her face. "You can talk to me about anything, you know. We're friends. Remember?"

She nodded and looked away. "Thanks."

He released her. "See you later," he said, and jogged away, leaving her wondering about the way he'd made her feel.

When she returned to the Inn, Charlie met her in the kitchen with an impish grin. "You going out with Austin tonight?"

Livy's gaze rested on Charlie. She was striking with long auburn hair and green eyes that were now lit with mischief. "Austin said that you and Brooke told him I was free tonight. How could I say no?"

Brooke walked into the kitchen. "Say no to what?"

"To Austin," said Charlotte. "He's taking her out to dinner tonight."

"About time you two got together," said Brooke. Not as tall as Charlie, and with short hair dyed purple, Brooke was as attractive in her own way. "What fancy place is he taking you to?"

"No fancy place," said Livy. "I chose The Crab Shack."

Brooke laughed. "That's perfect."

Livy frowned and studied her. "Why? What are you two planning?"

"Nothing," said Charlie.

"It's just that he's been dating a woman named Aynsley Lynch, and she'd never be seen in The Crab Shack. Heaven forbid. Not posh enough for her." Brooke shook her finger. "I warned Austin that Aynsley was just after his money, and he seemed surprised."

"Wow, Brooke, I can't believe you said anything like that to him," said Livy.

Charlotte gave Brooke a pat on the back. "Our Brooke is speaking up these days. All that freedom from worrying about her mother is giving her wings."

"And a mouth," said Brooke, laughing. "It's true. After climbing out of the rut I was in before coming here, I feel as if I can speak up."

"Gran's asking us to come help out at the Inn for the summer has been a gift to all of us," said Charlotte. "We're each finding our own way."

"And love too," said Livy. "At least for you two."

"Aw, Livy, it'll happen for you," said Charlie.

"I'm not sure what I want," said Livy truthfully. "But as the summer is progressing, I'm thinking more and more about making a change and staying in Florida."

"Dylan and I are seriously thinking of splitting time between Florida and Santa Fe," said Brooke. "We haven't worked out the details yet, but we will."

"And you all know that after Gran and John return, I'll be moving to Miami to be with Shane," said Charlotte.

They looked at one another and smiled.

"We just might be able to do it," said Charlotte. "Run the Inn with Gran and John. Even if it's part-time or from a distance, each of us can help in our own way."

Livy wished she didn't feel so overwhelmed and adrift. Knowing where she wanted to live was a start, but there were still many other decisions she needed to make. But then, how could she make choices for the future until she'd dealt with the baggage of her past?

###

That evening, Livy waited with a mixture of anticipation and dread for Austin to pick her up for dinner. Of all the men at the cove, he was the one she tried to avoid. He brought out conflicting feelings within her. He had her wanting things she wasn't ready for, and aroused feelings she couldn't deal with. Not yet.

His car pulled up to the back of Gran's house, and she went outside to greet him.

"Hi, Livy," he said, climbing out of the car. "You look great."

"Thanks," she said, happy she hadn't overdressed for the occasion. Her short denim skirt was comfortable. The light, frilly white top was another of her favorites. She had no intention of trying to compete with the women Austin had been seen with in the past.

Austin assisted her into his car and then took off down the coast to The Crab Shack, a favorite of locals and tourists alike.

When they pulled into the crowded parking lot, Austin said, "I'm glad I made reservations. Look at the line waiting to get inside."

Livy liked the notion of the restaurant being crowded. It meant talk wouldn't be necessary to fill any quiet between them. She knew Austin might ask her again about her tears that morning, and she didn't want to get into that discussion.

After she emerged from his car, Austin took her elbow and led her past the people waiting outside.

When Austin gave her his name, the hostess said brightly, "Right this way. I saved the spot you wanted." She led them to a corner table where they could get a view of the others in the crowded interior and gave them each a menu before she left.

Livy took a moment to glance around. It amused her to see adults wearing plastic bibs with a red lobster pictured on them. But they were needed if those people liked to dig into crabs the way she did. The room was filled with conversations as people enjoyed the casual atmosphere. Brown paper covering the tables along with the roll of paper towels atop each table contributed to the informality of The Crab Shack.

"I know I'm going to order the crab special. I get it every time. How about you, Livy?" said Austin. "Should we order beer, or would you rather have a cocktail or wine to begin?"

"Beer sounds perfect with the crab. I love a good IPA," she said, putting down her menu. "Like you, I'm getting the crab special."

He smiled at her, bringing out that devilish dimple of his. "You sure make it easy." He signaled the waitress, and they placed their orders. After their pitcher of beer came, he filled two chilled mugs and then lifted his mug in a toast. "Here's to a pleasant evening."

Smiling, Livy clinked her mug against his. "Thanks."

They each took a sip of beer and then Austin set his down. "I meant what I said this morning. I'll never forget your offer to sit in the front of the church facing me so I could focus on a friendly face while I spoke about my mother. It meant a lot to me."

"I was happy to do that for you," Livy said sincerely. "How are you doing with the aftermath of her death?"

Austin shrugged. "So-so. I'm talking to Shane's psychologist about the toxic relationship I had with my mother, and I'm trying to keep busy. As you know, I've been staying in Miami a lot, seeing old friends."

"Brooke told me you're dating Aynsley Lynch," Livy said.

"Yeah, Brooke doesn't like her. Told me flat out that Aynsley is interested only in my money." Austin chuckled. "Brooke's not the shy woman she once was."

"She admits it," said Livy, joining in his laughter. "This summer has been great for all of us. It's a chance of a lifetime for this many cove kids to be able to spend time together."

"Two engagements have come of it," said Austin. "How about you? Any romance in your life?"

She shook her head. "I'm not looking for any. The more important thing for me at the moment is to make some decisions about my new career direction. After owning a bakery for several years, I've decided I want to do something different. Grace Hendrix wants me to supply some baked goods to her restaurant, Gills, in Clearwater. That's a definite possibility. I haven't mentioned it to Charlie and Brooke, but in the meantime, I'm thinking of offering cooking lessons at the Inn."

"You sure are a great cook," said Austin, giving her a look of approval.

Their waitress arrived with a huge platter of steaming crab legs and melted butter and a basket of warm rolls. They tied plastic bibs around their necks and dug into the plate of crab legs. The sweet, tender crabmeat brought a murmur of pleasure from Livy.

Austin looked up at the sound and gave her a wink. "Tasty, huh?"

"Delicious," she said, dabbing at a bit of butter that dribbled past her lips. She didn't care. Getting messy was part of the fun of enjoying the meal.

Austin laughed, reached over, and swiped her chin with his napkin.

By the time, they'd finished their meals, their plates were mounded with soiled paper towels atop the empty crab shells, and the brown paper covering the table was stained here and there with the melted butter.

"I can't remember a more relaxed meal," said Austin, wearing a grin.

Livy returned his smile. Despite her doubts about spending time with him, she'd enjoyed it. Maybe a little too much.

"Do you want to stop by the Pink Pelican on our way home? Sitting outside with a cold beer is tempting," said Austin.

"A great way to end the evening," agreed Livy.

After he paid, they left the restaurant and climbed into his car, an Audi 5 convertible. "Do you mind if I put the top down?" Austin asked. "If you don't want me to, I won't."

"It's fine with me. It's such a beautiful evening, and the wind will feel good. Nothing is going to help these curls of mine." Her curly locks were constantly in disarray.

He reached over and patted her strawberry-blond curls. "I like them."

They took off, and as she suspected, the salty air cooled her skin as they drove through the dark to the Pink Pelican.

CHAPTER THREE

LIVY

At the bar, music filled the air with an exciting beat. Austin found a parking spot, and they walked into the bar.

"I'll be right back. I'm going to the ladies' room," Livy said. "Don't worry, I'll find you."

She hurried into the ladies' room, took a brush from her purse, and swiped it through her hair. Feeling better, she freshened and then went to join Austin.

Making her way through the crowd she searched inside the bar and then headed to the deck outside. She found him seated with three others, a dark-haired woman who had an arm draped across Austin's shoulder and two other people.

When Austin saw her, he stood. "Livy, come meet my friends. Everyone, this is my friend, Livy Winters."

She moved to his side as he indicated the dark-haired woman, who was stunning with classic features and dark, almost ebony eyes. Eyes that narrowed at the sight of her.

"This is Aynsley Lynch," said Austin.

Livy acknowledged her and turned to the others.

"This is Justin Schuyler and his wife, Izzy, the newlyweds in my Miami group of friends," Austin said with a surprising note of envy. Or maybe it was Livy's imagination, because his expression hardened when Aynsley pulled him down into the chair next to her.

Justin jumped up and dragged another chair over to the table. "Nice to meet you, Livy. Have a seat. Austin went ahead and ordered beers for all of us."

"Perfect," said Livy, smiling at Austin, though she wanted to leave. Aynsley was clinging to Austin as if he were going to fly away.

"How do you two know each other?" Aynsley asked her.

"We grew up spending summers visiting our families at Sanderling Cove," Livy said.

"Yeah, Livy's a cove kid," said Austin.

Aynsley clapped a hand to her forehead. "I'm so tired of hearing about the cove kids. You all stick together. It's impossible to talk to Austin when he's with any of you."

"Why don't we relax and enjoy ourselves," said Izzy. "We came over to this coast to do something different."

"I came here hoping to see Austin," purred Aynsley. She waggled a finger at him. "You haven't been returning my phone calls lately."

"I told you I was going to be busy setting up my office and developing a new computer program for work," said Austin.

"I'd love to go to your new little shack where you're setting up your office." Aynsley glanced at Livy. "Alone, and later."

Livy emitted a sigh and shook her head. The little shack Aynsley talked about was actually a nice beach house with three bedrooms and two baths. Not so little and certainly not a shack.

The beers Austin had ordered arrived, and everyone was quiet for a while.

"How about a dance, Austin?" said Aynsley.

He shook his head. "Sorry. I've saved this one for Livy." He stood and held out his hand to her.

Livy rose and took it, aware of the glares Aynsley cast at her.

They went out to the sand, hand in hand.

Livy kicked off her sandals and began to move to the beat of the music, trying to shake off her irritation at Aynsley.

Austin grinned at her, and they moved in tandem, letting the music carry them away.

When the song ended and a slow, romantic song began, Austin took hold of Livy's hand and pulled her to him. Once more, the music seeped inside Livy. When Austin drew her even closer, she rested her head against his broad chest, closed her eyes, and swayed to the music with him. For a moment, she allowed herself to enjoy the press of his body against hers, feeling a sense of rightness about it. She glanced up at Austin, and at the tenderness she saw on his face, she sighed happily.

When the music ended, Livy and Austin stood staring at one another, and Livy suspected he might be feeling the connection too.

Any thoughts of romantic interlude were shattered when Aynsley stepped between them.

"This next dance is mine," Aynsley said, smiling at Austin.

Austin gave Livy a helpless look and took Aynsley's hand as the band played another slow number.

Livy picked up her sandals, left Austin and Aynsley, and returned to the table.

An unfamiliar man was now part of the group. He stood when she approached. "Hi, I'm Daniel Cortane, Aynsley's date. I'm late, but I had a difficult time getting away from Miami. 'Didn't know there'd be six of us, but I'm glad. Would you like to dance?"

"Thanks, but I need to wait this one out," said Livy, fanning herself. "It's hot." She couldn't face dancing with a stranger this soon after that dance with Austin. Her emotions were still in overdrive from the way he'd made her feel.

Daniel said agreeably, "Maybe later, when it's cooled down."

"Yes," Livy said, relieved he wasn't persistent. They both

glanced at Aynsley, who was caressing the back of Austin's head and staring up at him with a broad, covetous smile.

"I've ordered another round of cold beers for everyone," said Daniel, nodding to the waitress who was setting beer bottles down on the table.

Austin and Aynsley returned a few minutes later.

"Ah, whoever ordered the beers, thanks," said Austin, picking up a bottle and holding it against his flushed cheeks.

"I had Daniel order them," said Aynsley, smiling at Austin.

Daniel turned to Livy. "Maybe we'll still have time for a dance."

Aynsley looked from Daniel to Livy and back to him. "What's going on? You're my date, Daniel."

He shrugged. "Just thought I'd ask Livy for a dance. She's already turned me down once, but I'm not one to give up easily."

Austin, who'd taken a seat next to Daniel, elbowed him. "Sorry, bud, but I get the next dance with Livy."

Aynsley shook her head. "It's charming that the cove kids are so kind to one another. Close *friends*, and all. Right, Livy?"

Livy heard the taunt in Aynsley's voice and ignored it, instead turning to Izzy. "If you and Justin haven't visited The Sanderling Cove Inn, you might want to come see where my family lives and works."

"Thank you," said Izzy. "That's something we plan on doing another time. We're staying at the Don Cesar in St. Pete Beach tonight. But Justin knows both Austin and Shane, and after talking to Shane, I'm excited to meet Charlotte and to see the Inn where you both work. There's a third cousin. Right?"

Livy smiled. "Yes, Brooke Weatherby is my other cousin. She handles a lot of the financial stuff while my grandparents are away."

"Are you going to stay on at the cove when they return?"

Izzy asked.

"I'm leaning in that direction. I'm a professional baker, and I have to decide how and where I want to proceed with my business."

"You should taste her baked goods," said Austin, smiling at Izzy and placing an arm across Livy's shoulders.

"It's hard to find decent help today, especially one who can cook," said Aynsley.

Izzy rolled her eyes at Livy but remained silent.

After a small break, the band started up again. "We've had a request for a couple of slow numbers. Looks like the full moon is playing a part in this evening," said one of the guys from the band. "Here goes!"

Austin turned to Livy. "One more?"

Livy got to her feet and slipped off her sandals.

"Let's all dance," Daniel said, and he and the others at the table rose.

Austin led Livy away from the crowd and put his arms around her. "I've wanted to dance with you like this again."

"Me, too," she said even as she warned herself to be careful. She still had so much to think about.

They swayed with the music, and once more, Livy laid her head against Austin's chest and heard the rapid beat of his heart. She knew he was feeling the same sexual tension that pulled at her. A shiver pulsed through her.

Austin looked down at her. "Are you all right?"

"Yes," she whispered, knowing it was a lie. She closed her eyes. She could admit it to no one else, but she'd been interested in him from the first day she arrived at the cove. But to be fair to him, she could only allow herself a few moments like this. Until she dealt with her past trauma, this was all she could give.

After the song ended, Austin lifted her chin and gazed at

her. "Livy ..."

She knew he wanted to kiss her and pulled away from him. "I can't." Before she could change her mind and give in to the temptation, she hurried back to their table.

"Livy!" said Austin, catching up to her. "What's wrong?"

"Nothing," Livy said, her heart beating so fast she thought she might faint.

"All right, let's go home," said Austin, giving her a look of concern.

Livy nodded, afraid to speak.

She picked up her sandals, grabbed her purse, and headed out of the bar, not waiting to see if Austin was following her. She had to get out of there, had to get some oxygen in her lungs, had to pull herself together.

Austin caught up with her as she approached his car.

He took hold of her arm to slow her down. "What's going on, Livy? You can tell me, I promise."

"Let's just go," she said, sliding into the passenger seat of the convertible.

"Okay, but we need to talk. How about I drive down the beach and park the car?" Austin said.

"No," she said. "Take me home." She knew she was shaking but could do nothing to hide it.

"Okay, then. How about going to my beach house?" said Austin. "I'm not sure what's going on with you, but I'm worried. I promise to listen to whatever it is that's bothering you."

Livy let out a long breath. "Okay." Everything within her said she could trust Austin, and she knew if she didn't tell someone, she'd explode.

They headed north on Gulf Drive. Not far from Sanderling Cove, Austin pulled into the driveway of what he called his beach house. The moon above them was a yellow orb in the dark sky casting a golden glow on them and their surroundings.

Austin helped her out of the car, took her elbow, and led her to a screened porch at the back of the house facing the water.

"Can I get you anything? A beer? Water? Coffee?"

"Coffee, please," she said, suddenly cold from a familiar fear. She wrapped her arms around herself. *Would she be able to do this?*

Austin returned in minutes and handed her a warm cup. Taking a seat in a chair next to the couch where she sat, he faced her. "Want to tell me what's going on?"

"Sometimes I get scared, that's all," said Livy, not sure she could bring herself to talk to him. He might think she'd blown the event out of proportion, that it was one of those "boys will be boys" things.

"Scared of what, Livy?" he said softly with such tenderness tears filled her eyes.

Livy took a moment to gather her courage. She sucked in a breath and stepped off the mental ledge with a giant leap of faith. "I had a really bad experience before I came to Gran's," she said. "I don't know what to do about it."

"Tell me," Austin said prompted her.

Livy looked away, wondering where to begin. Once again, she drew a deep breath and let it out slowly, reminding herself that it was getting harder and harder to hold the information inside.

"Everyone thinks I'm just someone who isn't serious about much except my job. But that isn't true. I'm more than someone who likes to have a good time with friends. I want everyone to believe that's who I am, but it's a cover-up. I haven't even told my cousins what happened to me." Austin sat patiently, holding her hand, waiting for her to continue.

Her eyes filled. "My ex-boyfriend is a teacher at VMI, an upstanding citizen who my mother thought was a great match for me," said Livy, not bothering to hide the contempt in her voice. "When we broke up, my mother was disappointed. I didn't tell her what led to our split. I was still too confused." She pulled her hand away.

"Too confused? What happened?"

Livy cupped her face in her hands and sobs ripped apart her insides and emerged from her throat in a wail she couldn't control.

Austin took her in his arms and held her while she wept. It was an ugly cry. She'd been hiding the truth from others, and it felt such a relief to finally let it out.

"He said it was my fault," she said between hiccupping sobs.

"My God! Are you talking about rape?" Austin asked.

"I fought him," said Livy. "The struggle ended when I managed to knee him in the balls. That made things worse. He screamed at me, grabbed me, and shook me so hard I couldn't breathe. He called me a cock tease and other awful names." She stared down at the floor as the memory of that violent night played in her mind, making her want to retch.

"I hope I never meet the bastard," said Austin in clipped, angry words as he held her tighter.

She pulled away and straightened to face him. "I thought we might have had a future together, but I wanted to take the time to really get to know him. Despite everything we had in common, it didn't feel right. He got tired of waiting. But a woman has the right to say no. I should be allowed to change my mind, shouldn't I?"

"Absolutely," said Austin. "No matter how much of a disappointment it might be to the guy, a woman has that right, and it should be respected."

"He made threats the next day, said if I ever told anyone what happened, he'd make my life miserable," Livy said sniffling. "That was the last message I got from him. Guess he was scared I'll report him or something."

"Maybe you should report him," said Austin, giving her a steady look.

She shook her head. "No, I never want to see or hear from him again. I just want to get over the idea that any guy can turn into a monster, pin me down, and try to force himself on me ..." She swallowed hard. "I just wish I could forget it. The night keeps replaying in my mind. Could I have done something different?"

"Stop. It wasn't your fault. Have you talked to a professional?" Austin asked. "I know how helpful that can be, trying to deal with my mother's death. I use the same counselor as Shane. I'm sure I can get you an appointment. Let me try."

"I guess I need to do that," said Livy, drawing in a shuddering breath. "I don't want to stay stuck like this. Thanks for listening to me. You're the best friend anyone could have."

Austin drew her close. "I'm here for you, Livy. Cove kids stick together."

Livy wanted to say much more but knew she wouldn't. She was still ashamed.

CHAPTER FOUR

BROOKE

Brooke was sitting in the office when the Inn's phone rang a few days later. She picked it up. "The Sanderling Cove Inn. Brooke Weatherby speaking. How may I help you?"

"This is Iris Sterling from *Coastal Lifestyle Magazine*. I've heard a lot about The Sanderling Cove Inn and the small weddings you're doing there, and I'm wondering if I can interview the three of you about an idea I have for an article on the Inn. Even possibly hosting a wedding there myself."

"That would be wonderful," said Brooke, feeling as if she could fly. This was exactly the kind of publicity they needed to grow the business. "When can you come here to meet with me and my cousins?"

"If it's not too inconvenient, perhaps we could meet later this morning," said Iris. "I need to see the property for myself and decide if this is something that would work to the benefit of all of us."

"Understood," said Brooke, willing to play the game of tit for tat. That's how a lot of business got done.

As soon as she hung up, she hurried to find her cousins. Charlotte was in the dining room talking to departing guests, so she kept on moving into the kitchen.

Billy Bob looked up at her from where he'd been scrubbing the counter.

"Is Livy here?" Brooke asked.

Billy Bob shook his head. "Gone on personal business."

Brooke frowned. It wasn't like Livy to take off without

telling either Charlotte or herself. She returned to the dining room and waited while Charlotte handed a map to the guests and wished them a pleasant day.

Charlotte turned to her. "Hi, what's up?"

Brooke felt a huge smile cross her face. "Something exciting. Listen to this." Brooke filled Charlotte in on Iris Sterling's proposal. "This could be huge for us."

"Yes, let's meet right now to discuss it. We want to be ready when Iris arrives," said Charlotte.

"Livy's not here. Billy Bob said she was away on personal business," Brooke said, feeling uneasy about it.

Charlotte gave her a surprised look. "Why wouldn't Livy tell us she was leaving? That's not like her."

Brooke shrugged. "I wasn't about to ask Billy Bob for more information. Guess we'll know what it's all about when she returns."

"Okay, let's go ahead and meet and come up with some ideas about how we want to present information about the Inn. If done right, this article could be helpful," said Charlotte.

Brooke was pleased that Charlotte was so talented at PR work. She'd done a great job of redoing the website and designing marketing brochures, giving the old promo items a new, fresh, more interesting look.

They each grabbed a cup of coffee and headed into the office.

Later, while they were compiling a list of notes to discuss with Iris, Livy appeared.

"Billy Bob told me you were looking for me," she said, pulling up a chair at Brooke's desk next to Charlotte.

Brooke filled her in on the upcoming meeting. "Charlie and I have been working on things to discuss with Iris."

"This is a wonderful opportunity for us," said Charlotte. "I'm hoping by the time Gran and John return, this Inn is doing better than they even dreamed it could."

"Me, too," said Livy. "The problem is the three of us are going to have to decide how we can continue to help even after they return."

Brooke studied Livy's face. Her upturned nose was sprinkled with freckles, her light-blue eyes were clear, and her strawberry-blond curls added to her charming appearance. There was an air of fragility about her that was more pronounced. "Is everything all right, Livy? You look ... I don't know ...sad."

Tears swam in Livy's eyes, but she shook her head. "I'm just working through a problem. I'm not ready to talk about it. When I am, I'll let you know. Thanks. Love you guys."

"You've been spending some time with Austin. Does he have anything to do with it?" Charlotte asked.

"Not really. He's just being a good friend," said Livy.

Charlotte started to say something, but Livy held up her hand to stop her.

Brooke's cell phone rang. *Her mother*. Relieved for the break in tension in the room she picked it up. "Hi, Mom."

Livy and Charlotte grew quiet and started to leave. Brooke waved them back. There was nothing she and her mother could talk about that wouldn't be appropriate in front of her cousins.

"How are you doing? How's Chet?" Her mother's nurse, Chet Brigham, was turning out to be a source of happiness for her single mother. They were dating openly now. And those who knew them were thrilled to see them together. Even from a distance, Brooke was aware of the changes in her mother due to the relationship and her better health.

They chatted briefly, and then Brooke ended the call and turned to her cousins. "Can you believe it? My mother and Chet in love. It makes me so happy."

"And now you can stop worrying about her and enjoy your own new love," said Livy.

"You and Dylan are great together," Charlotte said, smiling her.

Brooke returned the smile, feeling warm inside at the loving relationship she had with Dylan. She couldn't help glancing at the sparkling diamond ring on her left hand.

CHAPTER FIVE

CHARLOTTE

Charlotte focused on the elegant woman who'd entered the Inn. Iris Sterling was tall with a willowy body covered in a chic, sleeveless, brown-linen dress, and whose classic features formed a friendly smile that reached her blue eyes. Her gray, almost-white hair belied the youthful appearance of her lightly tanned skin. Pearl earrings on her earlobes matched the string of pearls around her neck.

Brooke and Livy moved forward with Charlotte to greet Iris. Charlotte hadn't had time to get a copy of the magazine in her hands, but she'd looked it up on the internet and was impressed. Iris made that impression grow stronger.

Brooke held out her hand. "Iris, I'm Brooke Weatherby. You and I spoke on the phone earlier today. And these are my cousins, Charlotte Bradford, and Olivia Winters. May we offer you something to drink before we adjourn to the office?"

Iris shook hands with each of them and said, "A glass of water would be lovely."

Livy went to get the water, and Charlotte followed Brooke and Iris into the office. They'd already arranged chairs in front of the desk where Charlotte would sit. Both Brooke and Livy agreed that she should run the meeting.

Charlotte took a seat behind the desk and waited for Livy to hand Iris a glass of ice water and take a seat before she began. "We understand you'd like to know more about the Inn, and we are delighted to have you here."

"Thank you, I've been hearing more and more about The Sanderling Cove Inn. It's taken on a new life with the three of you running it. I thought our readers would enjoy learning about the Inn, and selfishly, I think it would be the perfect place for my granddaughter to get married. It was she who mentioned it first."

"We love hearing news like that," said Charlotte. "What kind of wedding is your granddaughter looking for?"

"Something small, maybe on the beach, and with excellent food," said Iris. "We're going to limit the number of guests to as close to fifty as we can."

"We've got perfect locations around the property for wedding venues, including a gazebo, a garden, and the beach. As for food, you're looking at a skilled chef and baker." Charlotte indicated Livy with a tip of her head. "Livy's the best."

Livy returned their smiles. "I love to cook and can help make your granddaughter's wedding event delicious."

Iris laughed. "That's just what she's looking for." She studied Livy. "How is it you came to cook at your grandparents' Inn?"

"The bakery I owned with a friend in Virginia was recently sold, leaving me with lots of ideas about fresh starts. When Gran asked for my help, I was more than ready to come here."

Charlotte told Iris how she was frustrated at work and that her personal life was begging for a change. "Gran's request came at the perfect time. I was here first but it didn't take long for Brooke and Livy to arrive."

Brooke told about the need to get away from her hometown. "It's a fabulous opportunity."

Satisfied, Iris beamed at them. "I like the idea of you three coming together to help your grandparents. It makes an intriguing story. Now, tell me about your duties. Olivia, I know, is a cook and baker here. How about the two of you, Charlotte and Brooke?"

Charlotte explained that she'd been working at a marketing firm in New York before coming to Florida. Brooke told of her accounting experience, drawing more praise from Iris.

As conversation moved on, Charlotte wondered what was going on with Livy.

CHAPTER SIX

LIVY

Brooke and I will take Iris on a tour of the property," said Charlotte, getting to her feet. "We'll start with the dining area, the facilities, a guest room, and then head outside before ending the tour in the kitchen."

"All right," said Livy. "You go ahead. I'll prepare a few treats for lunch, if that's all right with you, Iris."

Iris beamed at her. "I was hoping to taste some food. Thank you."

After they left, Livy sat in the office thinking about her earlier meeting with Dr. Gleason, the psychologist Austin had arranged for her to meet.

A woman in her fifties, Dr. Gleason had suggested that a near rape was a traumatic event, and Livy shouldn't be ashamed or blame herself for Wayne's despicable behavior. That fact that he'd threatened her if she told anyone else was an attempt to control her and protect himself.

Wayne had stolen something that night. While he failed, Livy had to learn to trust intimacy with a man again. She'd been able to enjoy activities with the men at the cove in groups and the occasional date with Shane's law partner, Jed, but had never allowed any real intimacy with them. At least, understanding the difference between those she knew well and the man she'd thought she'd known was a big step forward. It was healthy to be cautious, but she also realized she couldn't deny herself a close, loving relationship because of that terrifying experience with Wayne.

Livy hurried into the kitchen to put together a fast, easy

lunch. Diced cold chicken was already in the refrigerator, and she set to work to create a curried chicken salad with pineapple. That, sliced tomatoes and crumbled gorgonzola napped with her special, homemade balsamic dressing, and some fresh French bread she'd had Billy Bob buy would make a flavorful lunch. She defrosted the frozen spice cupcakes she kept on hand for emergency occasions such as this and garnished them with a fresh dollop of fluffy cream cheese icing. It wasn't her best, but it would do nicely.

She and Mary Bowers, one of their kitchen helpers, quickly set a table in the small dining room with their good china dishes, crystal glassware, silver place settings and colorful linen napkins. A small bouquet of colorful hibiscus and lilies sat in the middle of the table. Charlotte had arranged an agreement that Tropi-Flowers would provide flowers for weddings at the Inn, and the owner, Rosalie Sweetwater, had been more than happy to deliver the bouquet for this occasion.

By the time Charlotte and Brooke entered the dining room with Iris, Livy was ready for them.

"This looks both beautiful and delicious," said Iris, taking a seat at the table. She gazed up at Livy. "Thank you for this last-minute preparation. I understand lunch is not normally served at the Inn except for weddings."

"This is something simple, but I hope it will give you the idea that we like fresh, different tastes," said Livy.

"In fact, we've drawn up a series of menu choices for brides," said Charlotte. "We'll be sure to add those to your information package to take with you."

"We remain flexible on requests, but it's best to start with something simple," added Livy, horrified by the thought of too many impossible choices for a crowd.

"Understandable," said Iris agreeably. "I think my granddaughter and her fiancé will love having a wedding here.

I've been assigned to scout the property first. But they'll make a trip of their own shortly."

"Let us know as soon as possible so we can give them a special pre-wedding rate," said Brooke.

"I'll tell them about it," said Iris. She dipped her fork into the chicken salad, chewed, and moaned with pleasure. "M-m-m, delicious."

Later, after the successful meal, Livy stood with her cousins bidding Iris goodbye.

As soon as Iris left, Brooke said, "Group hug for luck."

Livy laughed as her cousins threw their arms around her.

###

A short while later, Livy was cleaning up in the kitchen when Austin walked in.

"Any leftovers?" he asked with a teasing grin.

She responded with a soft laugh. "I saved some for you. Thank you again for driving me to Dr. Gleason's office and especially for introducing me to her earlier. I like her a lot."

His expression grew serious. "I respect her, too. She's been a big help to Shane and me."

Livy pulled a plate from the refrigerator and set it down on the counter in front of him. "Enjoy."

"Thanks. I was wondering if you'd like to go out tonight. Maybe go to Clearwater to Grace's restaurant, Gills. I haven't seen her and Belinda for a while, and I promised to talk to them about their wi-fi setup."

Livy hesitated and then said, "Sure, that would be fun. Cove kids helping cove kids."

A look of surprise crossed Austin's face. "Okay."

He finished his lunch and carried the plate over to the sink. "Thanks."

"You're welcome." Livy wanted to tell him how much his friendship meant to her, how much he was helping her deal with a bad situation, but she remained quiet. Best to go slowly as Dr. Gleason suggested. Still, she and Austin were cove kids, and that made a big difference. Without his support, she might not have found Dr. Gleason.

Austin gave her a wave. "Okay, see you tonight. Should we say seven o'clock?" He turned as Charlotte and Brooke walked in.

"You guys going out?" said Charlotte.

"It's business," said Livy. "Austin is talking to Grace and Belinda about wi-fi things, and I'm going to discuss with them the possibility of my baking selected items for their menu in the future."

"Oh," said Brooke, with a note of disappointment in her voice. "I thought it was a real date."

Livy didn't dare look at Austin. It wasn't a real date, was it?

"See you later," said Austin and left.

As soon as he was gone, Charlotte turned to her. "What's going on? You should've seen Austin's face when you said it was just business. Livy, I think he's really into you."

"You guys would be great together," Brooke nudged her. "Is that Aynsley woman still a problem? I don't know what he sees in her. He needs a wake-up call, and you just might be it, Livy."

"Aynsley is out to get him," said Livy. "That's for sure." The thought of him ending up with a woman like Aynsley sent acid to her stomach. But then, in her present state of being unable to make a commitment to him or anyone else, she should, in fairness, remain out of the picture.

"If it's okay with you two, I'm heading over to Miami for a couple of days," said Charlotte. "I'm not due to be here for the guests for a while. Is there anything else I need to do before I go? I'll have my computer and phone with me, of course."

"Go and enjoy yourself. How is the renovation on the house

coming along?" Brooke asked.

"It's not really renovation, more like total redecorating," said Charlotte. "No small feat. But both Shane and I are happy we're making the house the way we want."

"It was gorgeous before you started and will be even better with your personal touches," said Brooke.

"Can't wait to see it," said Livy.

"Austin is going to come help with a sound system for the entire house. Why don't you ride along with him one day?" said Charlotte with a sly grin.

"Charlie, stop teasing," said Livy, but she liked the idea.

Later, alone on the beach, Livy stood at the edge of the salty water and watched as a wave rolled in and pulled away after leaving what she thought of as a kiss. The top layer of sand beneath her feet followed the tug of the wave, exposing her painted toenails. She wiggled her toes in the sand and straightened to watch a trio of pelicans fly in formation several feet above the water, before the leader dove into the water and then came back to the surface with a fish in its beak, breaking the pattern.

She delighted in the bird life in the area. The fact that the Inn was named after one of the shorebirds was pleasing. A little group of sanderlings hurried by, their feet leaving prints in the wet sand behind them. She recalled a sweet story from her childhood of how even the littlest bird could trust in another day dawning. Maybe she needed to work on letting new days offer new possibilities. Ones that didn't dwell on bad memories.

With that decision made, Livy began to jog down the beach. For the first time since Wayne's attack, she didn't feel weighted down. She lifted her arms and twirled around, laughing for the pure joy of it. Life seemed good.

When Austin picked her up that evening, Livy was still in an upbeat mood. She'd kept to her pledge to try and heal from the past and move ahead. Being with a man she could trust to be a valued friend was another step in regaining what Wayne had stolen from her.

He greeted her with a smile. "Very nice."

"Thanks." She'd spent some time repolishing her nails and shampooing her hair. The new sundress she wore added to her satisfaction.

She and Austin chatted easily about things at the Inn and with the families at the cove. Having the grandkids spend the summer together was proving good for all of them. Love and genuine friendships were growing among them, much to their grandmothers' delight.

"Brooke asked me about Aynsley," Livy said. "She doesn't trust or like her."

Austin gave her a sheepish grin. "Brooke told me. The thing is, Aynsley's part of the group I hang out with in Miami. That's all. She and the others I grew up with helped me deal with my mother. I'll always be grateful to them."

Livy remained quiet, pleased that nothing serious was going on with Aynsley.

"As a matter of fact, next weekend I'll be staying in Miami," said Austin. "Several months ago, I promised Aynsley I'd accompany her to a charity ball—a fundraiser for a local cancer hospital. As I said, we're just friends, and I wouldn't break a promise."

They pulled into the restaurant's front circle and stopped at the valet station. A valet helped her out of the car, and she waited for Austin to join her before heading inside where a few people in the lobby were waiting to be seated.

After they checked in with the hostess, Grace walked into the lobby to greet them. A smile crossed Livy's face at the sight of her. Of medium height and with strong features like her brother, Dylan, Grace was more handsome than pretty. Her chestnut-brown hair offset her deep brown eyes beautifully. But it was the way Grace carried herself with confidence that Livy admired. Grace had been in her mid-teens when she came out. Her parents and the Sanderling Cove families supported her then and continued to do so after her marriage to Belinda. The two women were happy and worked well together making Gills restaurant successful.

"I'm glad you're here," said Grace, giving them kisses on both cheeks. "We just got in some sashimi-grade Ahi Tuna that's to die for. And Belinda made a truffle risotto that you'll love."

Livy's mouth watered at the suggestions. She knew everything served in the restaurant was carefully vetted by the owners.

Grace led them to a table in the corner of the smaller room of two, divided by a huge aquarium where brightly colored tropical fish swam furiously in circles or slowly glided in the sparkling, subtly lit water. Recessed ceiling lighting was supplemented by crystal sconces on the pale walls, shedding soft light about the rooms. White linen cloths covered the tables, offset by turquoise linen napkins and delicate, sea-colored glassware. In the center of the tables, candles flickered in crystal containers that held small seashells as well, enhancing the seaside theme.

Grace helped to seat Livy and turned to Austin. "You can hear the music through the speakers we've tucked into spots in the ceiling. We have a different system for the outdoor patio and in the bar. But we thought it would be better if we upgraded the system, making the same music play in all areas. I thought you could help us with that."

Austin bobbed his head. "Easy. No problem. It's something I can work on after I get back from Miami this weekend."

"We're closed on Mondays. That's a perfect time to do anything like that," said Grace. "Thanks, Austin. Be sure to order anything you want. We have some excellent champagne if you'd like. Everything is on the house."

She waved to someone walking into the room. "Sorry, I've got to go. Hostess with the 'mostess' and all that."

Livy chuckled and watched how easily Grace greeted others, no doubt making them feel special. Belinda, she knew, was handling the kitchen staff.

A waiter appeared with the wine list and menus. "Ms. Hendrix said you are her guests. She's suggesting a nice champagne for you. Is that something you'd like?"

Austin gave Livy a questioning look.

"I'd love it," said Livy. Sitting in a beautiful restaurant and being waited on was a treat.

"Sounds good," said Austin, nodding at the waiter.

"I'll bring that right to you and then tell you about our specials tonight." He smiled. "Ms. Hendrix told me she's already talked to you about the tuna. It's delicious."

After he left, Livy studied the menu. Most of the items were in the seafood category, but beef and chicken dishes were available too. She studied each course's offerings looking for new ideas, new blends of seasonings.

"Any thoughts on what you want?" Austin asked. "Or are you, like me, ready for one of each?"

Livy laughed. "I love looking through menus. But I'm going to go with Grace's suggestions."

"Me, too," said Austin. "If the owner recommends it, you know it's going to be tasty."

The waiter returned with a silver bucket filled with ice and a green bottle of champagne.

Livy loved life's pleasures of wonderful food and excellent wine. Maybe that's why her baking turned out so well. It was filled with the love of sharing it.

She watched as the waiter carefully removed the cage from the bottle top and then extracted the cork with a soft whisper. He waited for the bubbles to calm a moment before pouring the light-colored champagne into Austin's tulip glass for him to sample it. At Austin's nod of approval, he poured champagne into a glass for Livy and then refilled Austin's glass.

Giving them a little bow, the waiter said, "Enjoy. I'll return in a moment to take your orders."

Austin lifted his glass in a salute to Livy. "Here's to a nice evening."

Livy raised her glass. "Thanks for helping me, Austin. I appreciate it more than you know."

They clicked glasses and then each took a sip.

Livy held the bubbling liquid in her mouth for a moment before swallowing it. "Delicious," she murmured, "but then *Dom Perignon* is a favorite of mine. Being a foodie and in the hospitality business, I've been able to taste several different champagnes."

A shadow crossed Austin's face. "My mother liked champagne too."

"Your mother might have been difficult," said Livy, "but she had good taste. Charlie showed us pictures of some of the items she and Shane took from the house. They're beautiful."

Austin's lips curved. "I took a few things too. Sophia Morales, mom's assistant, insisted that both Shane and I have some of them. We're selling the rest."

"I didn't get much of a chance to look around at your beach

house, but from what I saw, it could be a beautiful place."

He lifted a corner of his eyebrow. "You really think so?"

"Yes. The setting is attractive and convenient to the rest of the coastline."

A soft sound of disapproval came from him. "Aynsley thinks it's awful."

"Well, I don't," said Livy. "It has a lot of great possibilities."

He studied her for a moment and then took another sip of champagne.

The waiter appeared, and though they listened politely to all the specials of the evening, they stuck with the choice of the ahi tuna special and truffle risotto.

As they sipped their champagne, they continued talking. Austin told Livy a little more about some of his friends and his life in California. In exchange, Livy spoke about culinary school and her role as a bakery shop owner.

"You don't want to run another bakery?" Austin asked her.

"Not as a full-time job," she said. "I love to bake but have realized I had little outside life when I owned the shop."

"I get it," said Austin. "Having the summer here between businesses has given me time to think along those lines too. But I need to be creative, to work. It's what I like to do."

"Exactly," said Livy. "My mother is into social things, volunteering and the like. But to be honest, I like making money."

He grinned at her. "You're so refreshing, Livy. I like it. You're not like a lot of the women I know."

She became serious. "After all that's happened to me, I'm being careful about keeping my independence."

"Understandable," said Austin. "I'm in no hurry to move into a relationship or a job situation I might not like either. I know Granny Liz would love to see me settle down with someone, but I'm not ready to do that."

"We should team up," said Livy, and then felt her cheeks grow hot as she wondered how Austin would react.

He laughed. "Team up to keep our grandmothers off our backs? Great idea. If they think it's real, they and everyone else will stop trying to fix us up. That'll be much better."

Livy was surprised by a stream of disappointment that washed through her at his quick response, but she laughed. She valued his friendship, and this was a way to handle the pressure that was being placed on them.

Their food came, and Livy savored each bite of her meal. She thought once more about possibly cooking dinners at the Inn if she decided to continue working there. They wouldn't have to serve dinner every night, maybe just on the weekends. She hadn't been kidding when she said she needed her independence.

"Delicious, huh?" said Austin. He patted his stomach. "I don't know about you, but I'm going to order dessert. You?"

She laughed. Austin made everything seem like fun.

CHAPTER SEVEN

ELLIE

Ellie looked at the words on the computer screen in front of her and beamed. Liz and the other women at the cove were convinced that Austin and Livy were becoming what they referred to as "an item." As old-fashioned as it sounded, it pleased Ellie. She read:

> **"You won't believe all the activity, Ellie. Charlie and Shane have bought a house and are doing some renovations to it. Brooke and Dylan are busy painting. Now that Brooke has sold a painting, she's really getting into experimenting with different styles, colors, and ideas. She's even signed up for a painting course.**
>
> **"As you can imagine, Karen is thrilled with all that's happening to her with two of her grandsons living at the cove. Of course, she loves being Mimi to Adam's little Skye which adds to her joy. Adam bought a fixer-upper house in case his new job doesn't work out and he sets up his own business flipping properties, but he seems happy to be here in Florida. Skye loves it here too.**
>
> **"Well, I suppose you and John are enjoying Scandinavia. It's hot here in Florida so being there sounds delightful.**
>
> **"Talk to you soon. We all miss you and John like crazy. *Skol*. Liz"**

Ellie shut the laptop and gazed out at the beautiful scenery as the cruise ship she and John were on made its way into a fjord on the coast of Norway. She was lucky, and she knew it.

CHAPTER EIGHT

LIVY

Livy sat with her cousins in the office at the Inn reviewing the weekly totals. Guest room sales were up, they had another wedding booked, and things seemed to be doing well.

"Any other issues?" Brooke asked, leading the meeting.

Livy cleared her throat. "I've been thinking about offering afternoon cooking lessons here at the Inn. They'd be open to our guests and to the people living in the area. What do you think?"

"When? What? And at what cost?" said Charlotte.

Laughing, Livy said, "Hold on, Charlie. One thing at a time. I was thinking Wednesday afternoons at two o'clock. I figure they'll last for two hours, and because it's during the heat of the day, it's a convenient time. I'd stick to baking and charge each person a fee per class. I'd limit each class to six people."

"Wouldn't we have to buy extra utensils, pans, and cooking supplies?" said Brooke. "If so, the cost of the class has to cover those expenses and more."

Livy was pleased her cousins were being businesslike. But she'd thought of all the details involved with holding the class. "I've already priced extra sheet pans, bowls, and such—all costs that can be covered over a matter of the four weeks before Gran and John return. The ingredients for each session would be covered too."

"What about your time, Livy? That's valuable too," said Charlotte smiling at her.

"Actually, my time would be well worth it in exchange for

the attention given to the Inn. And it will give me a better idea of what I want to do after the summer. Grace Hendrix has a friend who's a producer at one of the local television stations. I might be able to work up to having a program there. Right now, it would simply be doing something I love."

"Can we help in any way?" asked Brooke.

A smile crossed Livy's face. "Actually, I've already asked Billy Bob if he would be my assistant, and he said yes." Her expression became somber. "Not many people realize how lonely he is. He has his fishing boat and a friend or two, but no family. We've been working well together."

"Aw, Livy, that's really touching," said Charlotte. "I probably should sign up for your course."

"Not yet," said Livy. "I want to take care of guests and our neighbors first. If the course turns out to be successful, we might want to set up special programs and rates for our guests."

"You mean like a gourmet cooking or baking retreat?" said Brooke.

"Great idea," Charlotte said. "Something for the future. I like it. Does this mean you're staying at the Inn?"

Livy shook her head. "I honestly don't know."

"How'd your date with Austin go the other night? You looked really cute together," said Brooke.

Livy started to say they were just friends then stopped. If everyone wanted to pair them up, so be it. She and Austin knew it was just a ruse, but it would save them a lot of trouble. "Thanks. It was fun. We went to Gills and had delicious food."

"Sounds amazing. I'm glad you and Austin are getting together," said Charlotte. "Shane's been worried about Austin what with everything that's been going on with them."

Unsure what, if anything, she should say, Livy tried to think of a way to change the subject. "Speaking of Shane, when is he coming to the cove? Has he seen the fabric you want to use for your bedroom drapes?"

Charlotte grinned. "He's coming tonight. I can't wait to show him what the decorator and I have in mind for the master suite. I think he's going to like it. It's refreshing."

Now that everyone's attention was diverted, Livy rose. "I'm going to take a walk. See you later."

Livy headed down to the beach. She loved the opportunity to let her mind drift while walking the sand. She did a lot of soul-searching during these times, allowing the salt-air, the sound of the waves, and the cries of the birds to soothe her.

She was thinking of Austin and how he was helping her deal with the trauma of being victimized by Wayne. In addition to introducing her to Dr. Gleason, he was a sounding board to her after appointments. Having gone through counseling with Dr. Gleason himself, he was able to offer some insights.

As if she'd conjured him up, Austin came jogging up the beach toward her. She lifted her hand and waved.

Smiling, he approached her. "Out for a little fresh air?"

"Yes, it's a great way to think things through. By the way, just to let you know, Brooke and Charlie think we're together. I didn't mention that we're just friends; I let them believe otherwise."

"Good," said Austin, grinning at her. "Granny Liz thinks so too. Now wc can relax."

Adam strolled down the beach and approached them. "Hey, congrats, you two. Mimi just told me that you guys are together."

Livy blinked in surprise and cast a glance at Austin. He seemed as surprised as she, but stated calmly, "Yes, I guess you could say that." He slung an arm around Livy's shoulder.

She forced a smile. What had started out as a ploy, was

turning into a tricky situation.

"Anyone up for a night out?" said Austin. "I was thinking the Pink Pelican might be a way to relax. I'm going to Miami tomorrow, but tonight I can use a break."

"If we wouldn't be butting in, I'm up for an outing at the Pelican. Skye's preschool teacher and I were talking about going there earlier. Could we join you?"

"What do you say, Livy?" Austin gave her a questioning look. "Seven o'clock?"

"Sure, that'll be fun." Livy thought it was excellent timing. She and Austin needed to set new boundaries for their fake relationship.

Austin picked her up at Gran's house at seven. As Livy walked to his car, her heart did a little flutter. She told herself it was knowing she was safe with Austin. He was the person she'd trusted with her secret, and she knew he would never harm her. That was enough to make the evening special.

The Pink Pelican's parking lot was quickly filling when they arrived. Austin pulled into a parking spot and turned to her with a smile. "It's our lucky night. I think we got the last spot."

"I'm looking forward to having a relaxing evening," said Livy. "It makes it much easier not to have our cove families speculate about us. What will your Miami crew think? You'll be seeing them tomorrow."

Austin shrugged. "I don't care what they think. The only reason I'm going to this stuffy affair with Aynsley is to keep a promise. Nothing more."

"Okay," said Livy. She didn't want anyone prying into the scheme she and Austin had created. She needed to build up confidence in herself and trust in others.

Inside, they made their way through the crowd and onto

the outside deck.

Adam waved to them from a high-top table. Next to him, a black-haired woman gave them a bright smile.

As Livy approached, she could see that the woman had green eyes and a pert nose. She held out her hand. “Hi, I’m Livy Winters.”

“Nice to meet you. I’m Madison Mitchell.” As she shook hands, she gazed at Adam with an impish smile. “Better known as Skye’s pre-school teacher.”

Adam laughed and indicated Austin. “And this is my friend, Austin Ensley. Another of the cove kids I’ve been telling you about.”

Austin and Madison acknowledged one another with smiles, and then Austin and Livy took seats at the table.

Soft music played in the background. The live band wouldn’t show up until later. Livy was glad. The relative quiet gave them time to talk, and she was interested in knowing more about Madison.

Friendly, Madison soon supplied more information about herself. She had a daughter the same age as Skye and was divorced. She and Adam had decided to date casually to give themselves a break from being stuck at home as a single parent.

Livy liked how easy Madison was to be with and found she was enjoying herself as she told Madison about the work that she and her cousins were doing at The Sanderling Cove Inn.

Though not beautiful like Summer, Adam’s ex, Madison had irresistible charm. Livy was glad to see Adam’s pleasure in being with someone very open, so kind. Beauty was superficial. She’d been unimpressed with Summer when she’d recently met her.

They ordered drinks and favorite items from the menus the waitress handed them. Before the waitress left, Austin said,

"And I'll have the carrot cake on the menu. I want to see if you make it as good as Livy here. She's the best baker I know."

The waitress glanced from him to Livy with an amused smile. "Okay, I'll save you a piece of cake."

"You bake?" said Madison.

Livy nodded. "I used to have my own bakery. I'm not sure what I'm going to do now that I'm in Florida."

"That's why I wanted to order the cake," said Austin. "Maybe you could supply Gills with baked goods. Grace is dying to have you do some things for her. You could have a successful business without the hassle of being in a store all the time."

"Thanks," said Livy. "That's something I've been thinking about."

"I wish I could bake. I always seem to rush it, and my cakes are a flop," said Madison. "You should have seen my daughter's last birthday cake. It was delicious, though."

"I'm starting some cooking lessons at the Inn. Why don't you see about signing up? We could do a weekend course. Special discount for special friends."

Madison clapped her hands. "Really? I'd have to get a sitter, but I'd love to do it."

"Sari can play with Skye while you take the course," said Adam. "I'll watch her."

"That would be perfect," said Madison, beaming at Adam. "We can exchange babysitting."

From the way Adam was looking at Madison, Livy thought Adam was interested in exchanging more than that.

Adam stood. "While we wait for our food to show up, may I have this dance, Madison?"

"Of course," she said, smiling at him.

After they left, Austin reached over and clasped Livy's hand. "Maybe we'd better dance too."

"Oh, okay," said Livy. "We want to get into our fake couple roles."

Out on the sand, Livy kicked off her sandals and went into Austin's waiting arms, telling herself she shouldn't let romantic memories of an earlier dance with him affect how she felt now. But as they swayed to the music, she couldn't help resting her head on Austin's chest. It was how they fit together.

Austin rubbed her back. But as soon as the song ended, Austin pulled away and drew a deep breath. "Our food must be here by now."

"Yes, we should go back," said Livy telling herself not to be disappointed.

As they ate and talked, Livy was happy she'd agreed to join them. It gave her an opportunity to see Austin relaxed. She knew more than most what a difficult time he'd been going through.

When Adam and Madison left the table for another slow dance, Austin looked at her. "Want to dance?"

She hesitated. "I do, but if you don't, we don't have to. I think we've convinced Adam and Madison that we're together."

"Oh, well, then ..." He suddenly stood. "Let's do it anyway."

Livy rose, accepted his hand, and walked out on the sand with him once more, her pulse racing with anticipation. The live band was prepared to set up and this was the last chance they'd have to dance like this.

Austin gazed down at her and drew her into his arms. "I really like this idea of yours," he murmured into her ear. "It feels right, you know, pretending like this, keeping everyone from speculating about us. Now we can just enjoy being together. Right?"

"Yes, this is much easier," she said, and then chided herself for sounding a little breathy.

"Hey, you two," called Adam. "The music has stopped."

Livy and Austin jerked apart.

When Adam and Madison chuckled at them, Livy joined in. This pretending was getting harder and harder because she was falling for him.

Austin took hold of her hand, and they walked back to the table.

A short while later, Madison said, "Sorry to cut the evening short, but I have to leave. My babysitter can stay only so long."

"No problem," said Adam. "I'll be up early in the morning with Skye. We do our morning walk on the beach before breakfast."

"And I'm heading to Miami tomorrow," said Austin. "Duty calls."

"You're going to that fancy ball Shane told me about?" asked Adam.

"Yes. Hopefully that will be the last of the social events. I've been representing my mother at some of the charities, but I won't be doing that anymore."

Livy remained quiet but was happy to hear him say that. That role didn't seem right for him.

Austin led Livy to his car. "I think we should stop at my beach house to talk some more. There's something I want to tell you."

Livy gave him a quizzical look.

"I've done a little research and wanted to speak to you in private," Austin said, sounding mysterious.

"It's not something you can tell me now?" she said.

"It's better said with different surroundings," he replied, looking serious.

"All right. It's another beautiful evening, and I love your place."

They were both quiet as he made his way to his house and parked his car off to the side.

As Livy walked toward the front door, she made a mental note of what changes she'd make to it. Nothing too dramatic, just a different coat of paint and additional landscaping. But for what Austin was using it for, the house was perfect.

Austin unlocked the front door and ushered her inside, and then they walked to the screened-in porch at the back of the house.

"Can I get you anything? Water? Coke? Beer?" Austin asked her as she took a seat in one of the chairs.

"Nothing, thank you," said Livy, wondering what Austin wanted to talk to her about.

Austin sat in a chair and faced her. "Before I picked you up tonight, I did a little checking online about Wayne Chesterton and then with the help of an investigator. It seems you're not the only woman Wayne has abused. A woman in your old city of Lexington, Virginia, asked for a protection order against him and then rescinded it. I thought you ought to know. If you ever want to proceed with any legal action against him, you might find others willing to help."

A sickening feeling whirled through Livy. She grasped the arm rests with both hands and hung on, trying to maintain her balance. "As I've said before, I never want to see or hear from him again."

"Okay, I understand. I just didn't want you to keep thinking it was something you did or said. That man is a real creeper. Maybe the reporting incident will shake him up enough for him to change. My guess is he's going to remain a creeper."

"Thanks for caring so much. It's sweet of you. But I'm dealing with this in my own way with Dr. Gleason's help."

"I get it. I really do," said Austin. "It just makes me mad every time I think of you going through something like that."

Livy looked out at the moving water and let the sound of it calm her as it usually did.

"Let's go back to the cove. I know you have to get up early and so do I." Austin rose and helped her to her feet.

She looked up at him. "Thanks for watching out for me."

"I'm here for you, Livy. Let me know how I can help." He bent down and brushed her cheek with his lips.

Livy stepped away, afraid she might break down in his arms even as old memories resurfaced.

He took her elbow and led her outside. After locking his front door, he walked with her to his car, and they got in.

When they entered the cove, Livy breathed out a sigh of relief. This place had always been a haven to her.

CHAPTER NINE

CHARLOTTE

Charlotte signed the last set of documents and leaned back with a sigh of relief. It was official. She was now the proud owner of CB Publicity, LLC, in Miami, Florida. The house she and Shane were buying had plenty of room for an office for him and a larger one for her.

This was a big step for her, but it filled her with relief. Now, if Gran and John decided to keep the inn, she'd be able to continue to help them as part of her business. She'd already discussed this with Jake McDonnell, their financial advisor, getting advice about how best to handle the situation financially. She didn't want them to pay for any of her services. And if they sold the Inn, she'd petition the new owners to continue her work.

After Shane's colleague, who'd helped her with the legal documents, bid her goodbye, Charlotte sat for a moment, enjoying the idea of owning her own company.

Shane walked into the office. "How'd it go? Is it official?"

She smiled up into his handsome face. With his blond hair, blue eyes, and tanned, healthy body, he was the perfect model for living in Florida. "It is. All mine."

"Let's go celebrate," Shane said. "It's not every day someone starts a new company."

Charlotte let out a modest laugh. "It's a small beginning, but I'm optimistic about it."

"As you should be," Shane said, placing an arm around her and kissing her on the lips. "I'm proud of you, Charlie. Your work for my charity, Family First, is outstanding, and other people have noticed."

Charlotte smiled her thanks. Her work for Family First had helped form the idea of setting up her own company so she could stay in Florida. And after their engagement, she was determined to do it in a way that would benefit her grandparents. She'd be living in Miami but would be able to go to Sanderling Cove when needed.

One of their favorite restaurants was a neighborhood place called Luigi's. If someone didn't know about the delicious food served there, they might not be impressed. The exterior of the low-rise brick building was unassuming. Only the awning over the front door indicated a restaurant existed. That, and the mouth-watering aromas emanating from the building as one drew close.

Charlotte sat with Shane inside at a table for two feeling a sense of accomplishment. Between the purchase and redecorating of the house they'd bought and setting up her business, she'd been away from the Inn a lot recently. But with two upcoming weddings, she had to do her share and would be spending most of the next two weeks at the cove.

Shane ordered a Montepulciano red wine, and after he tasted and approved it, they watched as the wine steward poured some into each glass and left them to peruse their menus.

"What are you going to have?" Shane asked her. "I'm going with my favorite—spaghetti with house-made Bolognese sauce."

"I'm having the veal picatta," said Charlotte. "Love the lemon-and-caper butter sauce that goes with it."

"That's easy," said Shane, closing the menu. "Know how much I love you, Charlie?"

Charlotte's lips curved. He always made her feel special. His family, too, made her feel that way with their easy acceptance of her. She reached across the table and squeezed his wide hand. "I love you too."

"Hey, you two," came a voice. Charlotte looked up at Jed Jenkins, Shane's law partner.

"What are you doing here?" Shane asked him.

"Meeting up with a friend. Now that Livy and Austin are together, I've given up on her."

"I'm sorry it didn't work out for you," Charlotte said, aware he'd fallen for Livy.

"Yeah, well, those things happen," he said. Jed turned and waved at a redhead who was signaling him from another table. "Gotta go. Congrats on the new business, Charlie. I know it'll be a big success."

"Thanks," she replied, watching him make his way to his date.

"Speaking of Livy and Austin," Shane said. "I overheard Austin talking to Livy about some kind of appointment. I'm not sure what's going on, but I suspect they might be going to counseling."

Charlotte frowned. "Really? I would think Livy would tell Brooke and me about anything like that. I admit that until she and Austin were together, Livy seemed sad, offbeat somehow. I kept wanting to ask her about it, but the time never seemed right."

"I don't think it's anything to worry about," said Shane. "I just thought I'd mention it."

He lifted his wine glass. "Cheers!"

Charlotte raised her glass and clinked it against his, but she vowed to keep an eye on Livy.

CHAPTER TEN

LIVY

Livy and Brooke bid goodbye to Iris Sterling's granddaughter, Margo, and her fiancé, Cliff Dubois.

"They're a great couple," gushed Brooke. "And he's from your home state of Virginia. Love that little Southern drawl."

"Just a hint of it," said Livy. "You should hear some of my friends speak."

"Well, I like it, and I like them," said Brooke. "And I think their wedding is going to be adorable."

Margo and Cliff had decided to get married on the beach with a black and white theme, and wanted everything to be super fun, upscale in a comfortable way. The men would wear black shorts and white jackets; the two bridesmaids were wearing dresses in black and white floral patterns. The only colors would be with the flowers. Cliff's brother and a cousin would be the two groomsmen, and Margo's two best friends were going to be bridesmaids. The guests would be limited to 60 people, and thirty of the thirty-six guestrooms were being held for the wedding party.

"It's going to be a great wedding," Livy agreed. "I'm relieved they're sticking to one of the menus I put together for weddings. The menu selections are classic, a little showy, but tried and true."

"The wedding that will follow theirs isn't going to be as upscale, but it'll still be lovely," said Brooke. "I have to remember that each woman has an idea of what she wants for her wedding."

"Have you made any decisions about your own wedding?" Livy asked.

Brooke shook her head. "Nothing in particular except we want it to be small, maybe here at the cove."

"Charlie is thinking the same thing," said Livy. "The Inn is the perfect place for a wedding."

Brooke gave her a penetrating look. "Any idea what you and Austin will do?"

Livy was shocked and held up her hand to stop her. "Whoa! Austin isn't close to asking me to marry him, and neither am I ready for that."

"But you love him, don't you?" Brooke asked.

Livy drew a deep breath, wondering how best to answer and then decided truth was always the best policy. "He's everything I want in a husband one day."

Brooke continued to stare at her, one eyebrow raised.

He was trustworthy, the kind of man any woman would be proud to marry. Including her. "Okay, I love him," Livy admitted. Pretending they were a couple, she found herself looking forward to their almost-daily talks. He was such a steadying force in her life.

"I'm glad," Brooke said, unaware of the turmoil in Livy's mind. "Now let's get to work updating the information sheet for Margo's wedding."

They'd kept a strict accounting of each conversation with anyone connected to the wedding, copying the bride on each new addition to avoid any last minute snafus.

It was also a way to keep track of the inventory of items needed for the ceremony as well as the following reception. They'd increased the number of place settings of dishes and glassware and had purchased additional serving pieces and cookware with each wedding, their costs covered by the fees charged.

They were still in the office when Austin appeared. "Got a minute, Livy?"

"Sure," she said, wondering what he wanted. He looked a little frazzled after his weekend in Miami.

"Let's take a walk on the beach," said Austin. "I need to tell you something."

"Okay, it's a beautiful afternoon, and I need the exercise." She followed him out to the sand, kicked off her sandals, and stood in the water's edge, loving the feel of the salty kisses of the waves at her ankles.

Austin joined her and took hold of her hand. "When I was in Miami at the charity ball, I had my photo taken with Aynsley. I discovered today when the social magazine came out that Aynsley had referred to me as her fiancé. I called the magazine but there's nothing they can do about it."

"I thought she understood about us," said Livy, trying not to be angry. In reality, she and Austin weren't any more engaged than he and Aynsley.

"If anyone should mention it to you, just say it was an error or something," said Austin. "It's put me in an awkward position, but I don't want it to affect our relationship."

Livy saw the misery on his face. "No worries. We'll continue as we are. I understand it isn't your fault or your intention to be with Aynsley."

Austin sighed and shook his head. "She thinks I'm just going through a difficult phase and will come back to Miami and be with her."

Livy faced him. "I know you're at a crossroads, trying to decide where you want to live, what business you want to form, and other life decisions. I don't want to add to those complications."

The smile he gave her was filled with such tenderness that Livy's breath caught.

"You're a complication I want," he said. "We're doing this together, helping one another out. Don't change that, okay?"

"Okay," she said. There were times she suspected Austin really cared for her and other times when she was sure it was all part of their fake dating plan.

Mimi approached them, Skye in hand. "There are our newest lovers. It's nice to see you. Skye and I are collecting shells for Ellie and John's wedding gift."

"Oh, yes," said Livy. "It's such a special idea." She and the others in the cove were well informed about the collage Mimi and Skye were putting together with shells they'd collected. It wouldn't matter what the pattern was. Livy knew her grandparents would love it. This kind of gesture was what made life at the cove so precious.

Austin checked his watch. "I'd better go." He glanced at Mimi and turned to Livy with a questioning look. "See you later." He hesitated a fraction before giving her a kiss on the lips as if they usually kissed goodbye. Livy tried to hide the fluttering feeling inside her.

He winked at her before picking up his sandals and walking away.

"My!" said Mimi. "It does my heart good to see you young people in love. Adam said he had a great time with the two of you and Madison the other night. If only things would work out for him. He deserves to have someone special in his life."

Grateful to have the conversation focused on Adam, Livy said, "I think so too. Madison seems sweet, very kind. I liked her a lot."

"Sari's my best friend," said Skye, making them aware of her interest in what was being said.

"It's wonderful to have a best friend," said Livy. If she had to name *her* best friend, it would now be two—Charlotte and Brooke. At some point she'd have to tell them the truth about

Austin and her, but she wasn't ready to do that.

Margo and Cliff's approaching wedding gave Livy and her cousins lots to think about. Iris Sterling was someone intent on making everything perfect. In comparison, her granddaughter Margo was a free spirit. While Iris' appearance was almost severe with its conservative nature, Margo had tattoos and a nose ring that seemed suitable. Livy was amused by Margo's lack of concern about the particulars. She and Cliff were so much in love that details didn't matter to her. However, Livy was looking forward to being part of the process, making this wedding special.

Some guests on the bride's side arrived a couple of days early. Livy worked extra hard to make sure breakfast was handled well. There was already talk of other family weddings taking place at the Inn.

The day before the wedding, Livy was in the kitchen working when she heard a familiar voice say, "So it's true. You've reduced yourself to a cook in someone else's kitchen."

Livy gripped the edge of the countertop as she turned and looked into Wayne Chesterton's sneering face. "What are you doing here?" she asked, fighting to keep the tremor out of her voice. But she heard it, as did Billy Bob.

Billy Bob stepped forward and stood by her side. "You have no business being in the kitchen. Get out."

"Who are you to tell me to leave?" Wayne said, bristling. "Besides, it's my cousin's wedding so I'm a guest. You can't treat me rudely. It would be bad for the Inn's reputation."

A soft growl escaped Billy Bob's throat. He moved closer to Wayne.

Wayne's eyes widened. He stepped back and jabbed a finger at Livy. "You and I aren't over. We have unfinished business to take care of."

Livy wanted to stand up to him, wanted even to tell him to fuck off, but she stood gripping the countertop so hard her knuckles turned white. Her fingers dusted with flour were what held her up.

Billy Bob put a hand on her shoulder. "Get out. Now," he roared at Wayne, who hurried out of the room.

As soon as Wayne left, Livy collapsed against Billy Bob and held her face in her hands. Seeing Wayne was her worst nightmare. All the things she'd talked about with Dr. Gleason, the things she'd told Austin came flying back so strongly she felt as if her body had bruises from those punches.

"Hey, little lady," Billy Bob said softly, wrapping his arm around her. "I don't know what's going on, but don't you worry about that prick. I'm here. I'll protect you."

Hearing his soft words of comfort, Livy held on tight while he hugged her.

After she stopped crying, she stepped away and gazed up at Billy Bob. His unshaven beard, his crooked nose from a past fight were balanced by the kindness in his eyes. "Thanks for your help. It's an old, ugly story."

"I'm here for you," said Billy Bob, placing a gentle hand on her shoulder. "He won't dare come into the kitchen to bother you."

Livy nodded, too emotional to speak. For all his rough appearance and background, Billy Bob was a sweet man. She'd come to admire him. And now he was her hero.

"I need to go speak to Austin," Livy said. "Will you hold the fort here?"

"Sure thing. You go. I'll cover for you," said Billy Bob.

Livy was running toward Gran's house to get her car when

Charlotte called to her. Livy kept on going, consumed with the need to be with Austin. Her pulse was still racing at the memory of Wayne's mocking face, the look in his eyes that told her he wanted to hurt her again.

She drove away feeling the need to flee. Knowing Wayne was staying at the Inn sent paroxysms of nausea through her. How had she missed his name? Reviewing some of the guests listed on the daily sheet, she remembered seeing J. R. Chesterton. Wayne's full name was Wayne Chesterton, Jr. Maybe his family called him Junior or J. R.

When she drove into the driveway of Austin's beach house, she was relieved to see his automobile parked there. She pulled up beside it, got out of her car, and ran inside without bothering to knock.

He was sitting in the office working at his computer when she rushed inside. "It's Wayne! He's here staying at the Inn."

Austin jumped to his feet and shot her a worried look. "Are you all right?"

"No. I don't know. Seeing him brought it all back." She faced Austin and gave him a blank stare.

"What happened?" Austin said, coming to her and holding her close.

"He came into the kitchen and said something stupid like 'we have unfinished business.' The look he gave me was so demeaning. Thank God, Billy Bob was there. He told Wayne to leave and then he told me he'd keep me safe." Livy stopped talking and drew in a shaky breath.

"Do you want to call Dr. Gleason?" Austin asked.

Livy shook her head. "I know what I need to do. I just wanted to see you and know you're here for me."

He lifted her chin and stared into her eyes with a look of concern. "Always. You can depend on me." He hugged her to him and rubbed her back in caressing strokes. "I'd be happy to punch the crap out of that bastard for you, but that isn't going to take care of the situation."

"I know," Livy said. "I'm scared, but I'll stand up to him."

"I'd be happy to be there with you when you do," said Austin. "You shouldn't have to do it alone. Anyone in the cove family would be happy to help you. Me, most of all."

Fresh tears filled her eyes. She lifted her head, and when he lowered his lips to hers, she felt the anguish Wayne had caused ease a bit. She knew she wouldn't be free from him until she'd faced down her fear.

CHAPTER ELEVEN

LIVY

When she was composed, Livy left Austin's house and drove back to Gran's. She had work to do. The wedding couldn't be ruined because of seeing Wayne again.

Just before leaving for the Inn, Charlotte, Brooke, and Livy came together in the Gran's kitchen.

"Where were you going in such a rush earlier?" Charlotte asked her.

"I had to go see Austin. There's something you should know, but I can't discuss it now," said Livy. "Later, after the wedding, I'll tell you. In the meantime, we've got a wedding to oversee, and I want this one to be better than ever."

"Okay," said Charlotte, placing an arm around Livy for a quick hug. "We're here to help you through any problems."

"Absolutely," added Brooke.

Livy told herself not to cry. Her cove family meant everything to her.

They entered the gathering room each carrying a tray.

Livy scanned the room for Wayne, and when she saw him in a corner talking to people she eased out of the room and onto the lanai where other guests had gathered. She normally loved being able to meet the Inn's guests, but today was different. She'd had to convince herself that only by carrying on with her duties would she prove to Wayne how little he mattered to her now.

"Thought you could avoid me, huh?" came a voice behind her.

She whirled around determined to stand her ground. “Anything we had between us is over, Wayne. I have work to do. Stay out of my way. Now and forever.” She moved past him.

Wayne grabbed her shoulder. “You can’t run away from me like you did back then.”

She turned and stared in surprise as Austin approached, a steely look on his face. “My girlfriend told you she’s through with you. Don’t think for a minute you can bully her now like you did back then.”

“Stay out of it,” Wayne shouted and shoved Austin. Austin responded by grabbing Wayne by the arms to keep him away from Livy. As they wrestled and yelled at each other while trying to get an advantage, Austin hit Wayne on the chin. Then in the scuffle that followed, Wayne was thrown into the pool, his head narrowly missing the concrete edge of the pool.

“Hey! That’s my cousin,” said Cliff, joining them.

“Your cousin is a deeply disturbed man,” said Austin, brushing his hand across his cheek, catching a few drops of blood from his nose. “He can’t take no for an answer. Ask him about using his strength to take what a woman doesn’t want to give.”

“What?” Cliff frowned. “Are you saying ...” He glanced at his cousin in the pool and then back a Livy. “I didn’t know ...” He gave her an apologetic look.

“He’s an awful man,” said Livy. “One I hoped never to see again. I’m not the only one he’s abused.” She turned to Austin and taking a handful of napkins gently dabbed at his nose. She faced the crowd who’d gathered. “I’m sorry for the incident interrupting your social hour, but there comes a time when some people need to know what they did was wrong. Men shouldn’t get away with abusing women because they’re stronger.”

The crowd turned to watch Wayne climbing out of the swimming pool. Livy waited for him to say something, but Wayne just glared at her and at Austin by her side, shook his head, and left the area, his wet clothes leaving a trail of water behind him.

Charlotte and Brooke rushed to Livy's side.

"Thank you, Austin," said Brooke, looking flustered and teary-eyed. She wrapped an arm around Livy.

Charlotte hugged them both and then turned to the people crowded around them. "Time to get back to the party," and after moments of guests discussing the incident, the atmosphere began to return to normal.

Livy led Austin into the kitchen and put a cold compress on his nose to soothe the lump that had formed.

Studying his face, tears swam in her eyes. Without stopping to think about what it might mean, she whispered, "I love you, Austin. I know we're supposed to be just friends, but my feelings are so much stronger than that."

He set down the compress on the counter and drew her into his arms. "It was a silly scheme, huh? I've been in love with you for a long time."

She smiled at him. "Are you sure it wasn't my baking?"

He laughed. "Everything you cook is amazing, but you're even better."

They were still kissing when her cousins walked into the kitchen.

"What's going on?" Brooke asked. "Pushing guests into our pool isn't what we usually do."

"There's a lot you don't know," Livy said, becoming serious as she stepped away from Austin. "Wayne is my ex-boyfriend, and he tried to rape me a few months ago. He came into the kitchen earlier and threatened me. Billy Bob told him to get out. But I was able to tell Wayne myself that I never want to see him again, that whatever was once between us was gone." Livy shook her head and allowed a huge grin to cross her face. "Damn! But that felt good."

"That's awful," said Brooke. "It should never happen to anyone."

"If I'd known what he did, I would've pushed him into the pool, too," said Charlotte, her face flushed with anger. "Thank you, Austin."

Austin put an arm around Livy. "I'll make sure Wayne doesn't try to approach her again."

"Your nose," said Brooke. "It may be broken."

"I'm fine as long as I know he's not near Livy," said Austin, brushing away her concern.

"Do you mind if I explain the situation to Margo and Iris?" Charlotte asked her.

"No, I think we should," said Livy. "But I'm coming with you. Another way to face down the past."

"Excellent," said Charlotte, hugging her. "Gran would be proud of you."

"I'm proud of Livy too," said Austin. "Livy and I will remember this day for a lot of reasons." The look of love he gave her made her heart melt.

"Yes, we will," she said. Those special three words had been spoken, and she knew he meant them. Austin sent her such a tender look Livy caught the moment and hugged it to her.

A little later, Charlotte and Livy approached Iris and Margo, who were standing together.

"We'd like to explain," said Charlotte.

Margo waved away their concern. "You don't have to. One of my bridesmaids has already complained about J.R.'s aggressiveness. Like your boyfriend said, Livy, he's a scumbag who doesn't see women as individuals. Even Cliff is disgusted with him." She gave Livy an impish grin. "Austin is adorable, fighting for you like that."

"Yes, he's such a decent man," Livy said. This day marked a new beginning for her, for them.

"May we do anything special for you tonight?" Charlotte asked. "You have a group dinner at the Pink Pelican. We'll have coffee and tea on the buffet, along with a plate of cookies for those who want it later in the evening. Beer, water, and soft drinks are in the small refrigerator in the dining room."

"Excellent," said Iris. "Thank you for doing many extras to make this a charming affair."

"So far, everything's been great," Margo said.

After they left, Charlotte steered Livy into the office and texted Brooke to join them. "Time for a cousin talk."

Later, after Livy had told them the complete story and how she'd hoped living in Florida would help her move on, the three of them looked at one another and sighed.

"We've all found love here. Just like Gran and her friends had hoped," said Brooke. "Are we all going to stay in the area?"

"I know now that Austin and I love one another, but I don't think we're ready to be engaged. Austin has had a lot to deal with regarding his mother and her death," said Livy.

"Yes, Shane too," said Charlotte. "But I think it might be harder for Austin. He constantly went from being a hero to being brushed aside, while Shane always knew his place with her. Such a destructive woman."

"What about you, Brooke? Are you staying in the area?" Livy asked.

Brooke shrugged. "I don't know yet. Dylan and I have a lot to handle before that decision can be made. Like Livy, the only thing we know is that we love one another and will be married one day."

"Whoa!" said Livy. "All I know is that Austin loves me. Nothing more. A lot can happen before we start talking about making any wedding plans."

"True," said Brooke, "but I saw the way he looked at you. Still, we don't have much time to decide what we want to do about our future with the Inn. Luckily, Charlie already knows."

The next day flew by, every moment leading to the late afternoon moment on the beach when Margo and Cliff exchanged vows in front of their guests.

The simple black and white theme with colorful tropical flowers was stunning. Rosalie from Tropi-Flowers had decorated the small white tent set up for the ceremony with ropes of hibiscus blooms in red, yellow, purple, pink, and white. In contrast, Margo carried a bouquet of white lilies.

The photographer they'd hired was everywhere, taking photos for personal use and for Iris' magazine. Iris had promised plenty of photos for the Inn's website and PR materials.

Livy kept her distance but was relieved when Wayne left right after the ceremony, not even staying for the dinner afterwards. Wayne's father was particularly angry with his son and tried to apologize. It was an awkward moment for both of them.

Dinner was a successful affair with delicious food, excellent wine, and plenty of congenial conversation. Livy paid attention to details, storing some of them away for the day when she might plan her own wedding. She and Austin spent every moment they could together,

Guests were still lounging on the lanai at midnight when Livy made her way back to Gran's. Though she had to get up early to make breakfast, she hadn't wanted to leave such a happy, loving group. For the first time in a long while, she felt both secure about her future and free to do as she wished without the baggage she'd been carrying.

CHAPTER TWELVE

BROOKE

Brooke and Dylan walked the beach together, quiet but at peace. Dylan had gone through a spurt of creativity, working on beach scenes in bold, abstract strokes. Brooke thought they were some of his best pieces yet.

"All because of you," he'd told her, kissing her.

Now, he took hold of her hand and squeezed it. "You look lost in thought. What is it?"

"It's Livy and the fact that she'd lived with her situation for so long without telling anyone. Livy isn't that big a person. Wayne is massive by comparison. The thought of him trying to overpower her ... She must have been scared out of her mind. And then for him to be nasty about it?" She shook her head. "He's a horrible person."

"He must not have appeared that way," said Dylan. "Or else Livy wouldn't have chosen him. Right?"

"Yes. I think her mother thought he was a good choice for her, but she didn't know the real person. He's fooled a lot of people." Her voice softened. "I feel very lucky to have found you."

He grinned. "I feel the same. Any news from your mother?"

"Oh, yes," Brooke said. "It's all great." She didn't feel forced to call her mother anymore. They talked whenever they wanted, but not as often as in the past. However, with her mother having fallen in love with the nurse taking care of her, conversations with her were fun. Her mother seemed truly happy. "I'm wondering if she and Chet are going to get married. But I don't dare ask. I want that to come from them, not me."

"I haven't told you, but I talked to her the other day." Dylan smiled. "She called to see how things are going, and we chatted for a few minutes. She knows how important it is for you to feel free from the past and your taking care of her, and she wanted to check in."

"I know she misses me, but I'm pleased I'm here and very glad that she and Chet are compatible. It's such a relief to know how happy she is."

"My mother also called me." He squeezed her hand again. "She's crazy about you. My father, too. But then, so am I."

They stopped walking and turned to face each other. When his lips came down on hers, Brooke responded, seeing bright colors flash in her mind as his kiss deepened. It would always be that way for her. Love and color. He'd opened up her life to love and her artistic soul.

CHAPTER THIRTEEN

LIVY

Livy and Austin sat on the porch of his beach house, cuddled on the couch. Since declaring their love for one another, they couldn't seem to get enough time together. Their conversations deepened, making it easy to talk about almost anything. The one line they hadn't crossed was making love. They'd come close, but each time, Livy froze. Recognizing her discomfort, Austin had backed away. Now, though, Livy was determined to prove to Austin that she not only loved him but trusted him.

"I like when you cook dinner for me," said Austin, drawing her close. "It wasn't until I went to a friend's house when I was very young that I realized families usually ate together. Mine never did."

"Not even when your parents were still together?" she said.

"No, my father worked late, and my mother would go ahead and feed Shane and me before he came home. And later, my mother and Ricardo usually went out to some social event or for his business. Weird, huh?"

"Yes, too bad, really. But then, with my younger brothers going into sports, that happened to us too. Nobody on the same schedule. But my mother made us eat Sunday dinner together."

"Sunday was the cook's day off, so we just made sandwiches or got pizza," said Austin.

"Sorry, but that sounds awful. I want to continue to have family Sunday dinners," said Livy. "You know, when it's time to decide those things."

He kissed her. "You make me happy. I'd like to have a lot of kids. How about you?"

"Three is nice," she said. "It depends on a number of things."

"Like what?" he said, rubbing her back.

"Like family and work commitments," she answered honestly.

He sat up straighter. "Have you decided what you're going to do about the Inn?"

She shook her head. "No, but I'm sure Gran will want to know when she gets back."

"Do you see us together always?" Austin asked softly.

Livy heard the need in his voice and clasped his face between her palms. "I love you, Austin. I'm not going anywhere."

"Love you, too," he said lowering his lips to hers, filling her with desire and the need to prove that to him.

They kissed until she was full of such need that she could hardly breathe. It was now or never. She had to let go of the past to have a whole new beginning.

Livy stood and took his hand. "Come with me."

"Are you sure?" he asked, his face flushed with desire.

She gazed into his eyes, full of concern, and smiled.

Inside the bedroom, she stood awkwardly. She wanted him, yet needed to know he wouldn't make her feel trapped.

Austin lifted her into his arms and settled her on top of the king-size bed. "We'll take our time," he whispered in her ear. "Trust me."

"I do." She lay next to him facing him.

Austin kissed her and said softly, "I'll help you." He eased her top off, then stood, and took off his clothes while she removed hers.

In the dim light, she faced him.

His hands cupped her face and then he kissed her, sweeping away the last of her fears.

Later, lying beside him, she let the tears that had formed in her eyes leak onto her cheeks.

"Hey," Austin said softly, thumbing the tears off her face. "I didn't hurt you, did I?

"No," she said, drawing him closer. "You made me feel cherished. And so very happy."

"I love you, Livy, and I always will," murmured Austin, eager to show her once more.

###

The next morning, Livy rose quietly so she wouldn't disturb Austin, then remembered it was her day off, and Billy Bob was handling the kitchen. She slid back under the covers, not bothering with clothes and lay on her back staring up at the ceiling fan moving slowly above her. She'd never experienced the depth of emotion she and Austin shared. They knew how vulnerable the other was, and instead of making it awkward, it made the giving sweeter.

"Hey, there," murmured Austin, pulling her to him.

They made love all over again and then Austin said, "I'm hungry. How about you?"

Livy laughed. "Starving. C'mon, I'll make breakfast."

Austin grinned. "A sexy angel who cooks. How lucky can a guy be?"

When Livy returned to the Inn, Brooke met her in the office. "Missed you this morning, but then I realized you were with Austin. How are things going?"

"Great," Livy said, unable to hold back a smile. "It's amazing how close we've become. We can talk about anything and everything. It's really special."

"I think the two of you are perfect together. Remember when you were a teenager with a crush on him?" said Brooke. "It seems as if it was meant to be all along."

"Thanks. If you had said anything like that a year ago, I would've laughed in your face. But I believe it now," said Livy.

She and Brooke discussed events for the day, and then Brooke left. Alone in the office, she lifted the phone to call her mother. They got along fine, though Livy sometimes felt pressure from her mother to find a man, settle down, and raise a family. Until she and Austin had been together, she hadn't wanted it. Now, having Austin's babies was something she was looking forward to in the future.

Her mother answered on the fourth ring. "Hello, honey. How are you? It's almost time for you to be done with your summer commitment. Have you decided on anything yet?"

"Hi, Mom. We still have time before any decision will be made about the Inn. Gran and John don't get back for another few weeks. But, Mom, I'm so happy I had to call you. I'm in love."

"In love? That's wonderful. Who's the lucky young man?"

"Austin Ensley."

"Henry's son?" her mother asked.

"His youngest son. Shane is older than he is. I think you're going to love him too. Austin's amazing, caring, so ... incredible."

"Oh, my darling, I'm happy for you. Henry was always one of my cove kids favorites. But I remember that awful woman who was his first wife."

"Yes, that would be Austin's mother. She died this summer."

"Well, I'm sorry for his loss. When are we going to meet Austin? I know. I'll have a special garden party to introduce him to our friends. I can't wait to tell Maribelle the news. I want every detail. I know she'll be pleased for me. What does he look like? How did you fall in love?"

"All in time," said Livy, suddenly unwilling to share the particulars. Though her relationship with Austin was real, it was new, and she didn't want to say anything to interfere with the happy glow inside her. Her mother would push too hard, too soon for a wedding.

"Okay, Olivia, I'll be patient, but not for long. This is big news, and I want to share it."

Livy sighed. "I just wanted to tell you about it. We'll talk later."

"Send me pictures and more information. I'll be waiting for them. Now, I'm off to the tennis court. My team is doing well this summer."

"Good luck! Love you, Mom," said Livy.

"I love you too, sweet girl. I've missed having you closer." Her mother blew a kiss into her phone.

The sound of it made Livy smile.

###

That evening after socializing with the guests, Livy met Austin in front of Granny Liz's house. Liz had decided it was time for another beach party, and Mimi and Grandma Karen were helping her.

It was a beautiful evening. The setting sun was an orange globe just beginning to lower behind the horizon. Livy, like everyone else at the party, was quiet as they watched, hoping to see the green flash. Livy never tired of looking for it. If certain things in the atmosphere were aligned, a green flash of light followed the dip of the sun from view.

Austin stood with an arm around her shoulder. "Guess it's not going to happen tonight. But I get a kiss anyway, right?"

Livy laughed and lifted her face to him.

His lips met hers, and the magic of this moment

outweighed any desire to see the green flash or anything else.

"Hey, all," said Adam, "Anyone up for a volleyball game on the beach?"

A group gathered around him, including Madison.

Austin turned to Livy. "You up for it?"

"Sure," Livy said. She was on the short side but had played for her high school team. Like everyone else, she kicked off her sandals and headed for the sand where a volleyball net had been set up for the families' use.

Seeing her cousins and all her cove friends together gave Livy a warm feeling. She recalled previous visits and realized how precious this time together was. For her cousins and her, this summer had helped guide them into making plans and meeting long-term goals. As for herself, she couldn't be happier. After feeling adrift and so afraid, she felt like a new person with a healthy choice of plans for the future.

The volleyball game was fun and full of laughs. As he'd been at a younger age, Adam was a natural leader and excellent sportsman. But Livy was surprised how others held their own against him. Even Brooke, who'd claimed she'd never really played much volleyball, did a satisfactory job of returning a ball.

After a while, eager to cool off, they settled on the grass in a group drinking water, sodas, or beer.

Granny Liz joined them. "We're about ready to put the food out. Everyone ready?"

She laughed at the chorus of yeses. "Okay, then, give us about ten minutes and come help yourselves. After dinner we'll start the bonfire."

Livy loved how the grandparents in the cove kept things going for the younger generations. It kept all ages involved.

###

Later, Austin asked if Livy wanted to go with him to his

beach house. She quickly said yes. She loved being with him there, where they could talk, make love, and she could dream of a time when they might be together always.

Austin drove into the driveway of his house and pulled to a stop beside a white BMW convertible.

"Who's here?" Livy asked.

Austin turned to her. "Looks like Aynsley's car."

"What is she doing here?" asked Livy, wondering at his look of disgust.

"I don't know. I've told her I'm not interested in a relationship with her, that I'm with you."

They got out of the car and walked to the front door. The lights were off except for the hanging fixture above the outside entry.

Austin unlocked the front door and flicked on the inside lights. From out on the lanai a figure rose and walked toward them.

Looking as if she'd just awakened, Aynsley approached. "Oh, good. The girlfriend is here. That'll make it easier."

"Make what easier, Aynsley?" Austin asked in a controlled voice. "I don't like people breaking into my house."

"Not even to deliver you happy news?" Aynsley wrapped an arm around him. "Besides, I didn't break in: I just walked around your house to the back and sat on the lanai. I think you'll be pleased. Like I said, I've got happy news."

Austin frowned. "What are you talking about?"

Aynsley gave him a satisfied smile. "I'm pregnant."

"What does that have to do with me?" Austin asked, lifting her arm off him.

Aynsley waggled a finger at him. "Don't you remember that night about two months ago when you stayed over?"

"I just slept on your couch," Austin said.

"So, *you* say," said Aynsley. She patted her stomach. "I

have proof that it was more than that." She gave Livy a smug look. "Sorry, but Austin is mine."

"No, I'm not," said Austin firmly. "You know it. I'm not sure what's going on, but nothing is changing between us, Aynsley. Nothing."

"But if the baby is yours?" said Aynsley in a wheedling voice that was like listening to a fingernail being scraped across a chalkboard.

"You know that isn't possible, and so do I." He pointed to the door. "Leave. Now."

"This isn't over, Austin. I'm going to demand a DNA test and then I'll prove it to you. In the meantime, don't make any wedding plans with your cove friend."

"You'd better leave now," said Austin ushering Aynsley out of the house.

Livy sank onto the couch in the living room, trying desperately not to throw up. She'd finally opened her heart to love, had trusted Austin in a way she'd never trusted a man before.

Austin returned and sat down beside her. "I'm sorry, Livy."

"Did you spend the night with her a couple of months ago?"

"Yes, I spent the night at her condo, but it's not what you think. After one of those horrible social affairs, we went to her condo, had some more drinks, and that's all I remember of that evening. I woke up on the couch with a pounding headache and figured I must've passed out, though I normally don't drink much."

"You didn't go to bed with her?" Livy asked.

"Not that I remember. Even though we weren't together, I'd already fallen for you. But things were messed up with my mother about then, and I didn't think you saw me other than as a friend. But I didn't do what Aynsley's accusing me of." He took hold of her hand and gazed into her eyes steadily. "You believe me, don't you?"

"I want to," Livy said honestly. "But what if something did happen that night and the baby is yours?"

Austin held up his hand. "Stop! I don't even want to go there."

Livy leaned forward. "Tell me again about that night. You went to a social event, went to Aynsley's apartment, had drinks, and then nothing?"

"Yeah, that's pretty much it. I don't remember that evening. I've never had anything like that happen to me before or since. Like I said, I usually don't drink much because of my experiences with my mother."

Livy's thoughts raced. Aynsley was enamored of Austin and his money, hated the idea he'd found someone else, and might be desperate. "This is going to sound loony," she said, "but is Aynsley in some kind of financial trouble? She was recently divorced. Right?"

"Yes. She left her husband several months ago when he lost a lot of money in a marketing scheme, then got involved with another woman. That's what she told me. They lost the house they were living in, and she's now staying in a friend's condo."

"Okay," said Livy. "I think it's fair to say the idea of Aynsley trying to involve you isn't as farfetched as one might think."

"So, you believe me?" said Austin.

"Yes, I do," said Livy giving him a steady look. "We're going to take this one step at a time. Together." After all that Austin had done for her, there was no way she'd desert him. She'd stand by his side and see him through this.

"Thanks." Austin closed his eyes, but not before she saw the tears swimming in them.

She hugged him, her own tears overflowing. She didn't like the idea of a future tied to Aynsley in any way, but she wouldn't abandon Austin. He'd helped her start the healing process from Wayne's abuse.

Austin drew her closer. "What a frickin' mess."

"We don't even know if it is," said Livy, leaning against his broad chest. "We'll have more facts in time. In the meantime, let's keep quiet about this until we get things straightened out. There's so much we don't know."

Austin cupped her face in his hands and stared into her eyes. "I've said 'I love you' before, but I've never said it with this much meaning. I love you, Livy, and I always will."

"I love you too," she murmured as his lips met hers.

A new tenderness filled Livy. She'd depended on Austin, and now he was depending on her. It took their relationship to a whole different level.

CHAPTER FOURTEEN

LIVY

With Austin in Miami trying to figure out how best to handle the situation with Aynsley, Livy was determined to keep to her schedule. Her first cooking lesson was set for that afternoon, and she was relieved she wouldn't have any down time to let the worries in her head continue to grow.

"Are you okay?" Brooke asked her, coming into the kitchen. "You seem a little down."

"Just a few problems to work out in my head. Are you ready to help Billy Bob and me with my first cooking lesson?"

"Yes. It's a great idea. The small group of people who've decided to join are thrilled with the idea of learning to make a carrot cake from scratch. I hadn't realized how many people just use a cake mix. But from what these ladies told me, they're eager to learn the difference."

"It's a substantial difference," said Livy. "But it's not for people who don't love to eat. We use fresh carrots and lots of butter and eggs."

The four people who signed up came into the kitchen chatting happily. A retired husband-and-wife team in the neighborhood joined two female guests.

Billy Bob, bless his heart, had put on a fresh T-shirt and apron for the event. Livy introduced him and Brooke and then handed out the recipe she'd printed up. She'd made so many carrot cakes in her career she didn't need a recipe, but she wanted her students to be able to follow along.

First of all, she made sure that each person had their ingredients at their station.

"I like using all-purpose flour, but you can substitute whole wheat, white whole wheat flour, or a gluten-free flour blend for some of the all-purpose flour," Livy explained. "We use baking soda, which helps the cake to rise. The cake doesn't need baking powder because we're using buttermilk, which will react well with the baking soda."

Livy indicated the little bowls of sugar at each place. "Sugar makes the cake moist, light, and delicious. You can use a combination of white and brown sugar, or you can use one or the other. Eggs give the cake structure, and lots of carrots make this the best carrot cake. We will hand grate the carrots for the texture instead of using a food processor. We will use three cups of grated carrots. Pecans and raisins are optional, but we've placed both at your stations."

"How do I start?" asked a young newlywed who was a guest.

"I like to keep dry ingredients in one bowl, wet ingredients in another," said Livy. "We make sure each is blended well before folding the dry ingredients into the wet. But let's peel and grate the carrots first and set them aside."

Billy Bob worked with the retired couple, Livy helped the newlywed woman, and Brooke helped an older guest.

As they worked, Livy talked to each individual, learning more about them as they grated, mixed, and blended. By the time the cakes went into the oven, it had become a friendly group.

"The cakes will take thirty-five to forty minutes," said Livy. "During that time, we can make the icing. The extra-creamy cream cheese frosting is a favorite of mine. I use it for one of my chocolate cakes. It consists of just three ingredients. Cream cheese, powdered sugar, and heavy cream."

"Can we lick the bowl?" the gentleman asked.

Livy laughed. "Of course. A baker has many privileges."

Brooke and Billy Bob went to work washing dishes while the students made their icing, tasting as they went.

When that was done, Livy offered lemonade, water, sodas, and coffee to the group. They sat at the kitchen table in the corner of the room and chatted easily with one another.

The newlywed, a pretty young woman from upstate New York, turned to Livy. "You ought to do a bachelorette party weekend for brides-to-be with an emphasis on cooking classes. We spent a lot of money going to New York City for mine, but after being at the Inn, I would have preferred coming here."

"I heard that," said Brooke, joining them. "It's something to think about. Room accommodations might be an issue, but even so, Livy could do cooking lessons here."

Livy liked the idea. Too restless to continue sitting, she rose and bustled around the kitchen. Her thoughts flew to Austin and his problem with Aynsley.

"I think the cakes are ready," said Brooke approaching her.

"Thanks." She turned to the group. "Okay, everyone. Let's pull the cakes out to cool. And while we're waiting, we can take a break. Then the fun of icing the layers will begin."

After the commotion of getting the cakes out onto the counter to cool, Brooke suggested that the four students take a short walk on the beach with her.

Left alone in the kitchen with Billy Bob, Livy turned to him. "Thanks for your help. I can finish this last bit by myself. It's a beautiful afternoon and I know you like being on your boat."

He grinned. "Yeah, she's a beauty. Maybe you could see it sometime."

"I hope I can," Livy replied, and couldn't stop tears from filling her eyes at his thoughtfulness.

"You okay?" Billy Bob asked, placing a hand on her shoulder.

Embarrassed by her sentimentality, Livy quickly wiped away the tears.

"It isn't that creep I had to chase out of here, is it?" Billy Bob's look of concern almost prompted more tears, but she blinked them back.

"No, but thanks. I appreciate your asking." She looked up at his weathered face, his worn features. He'd frightened her at first, but she knew him as a gentle giant.

"Okay, then. I'm going. I'll see you tomorrow morning." Billy Bob gathered his things and left.

Livy dashed into the ladies' room and put a cold compress on her face, telling herself no matter how worried she was about Austin, she couldn't fall apart. Though she and Austin had a lot to resolve, it wouldn't happen overnight. In the meantime, she had to do her job.

When the cooking class reconvened, there was a lot of laughter as the four class members spread icing on the cakes. Only one student broke one of the cake layers trying to place one on top of another.

Livy quickly showed her how to fill the crack in with icing by adding a few extra swirls. "You can also add raisins on top to detract from the crack. Believe me, when someone tastes this cake, appearance will be of little concern as they dig in."

"I want my husband to see this cake," said the newlywed. "Then I'll offer it to anyone at the Inn."

"You're welcome to take it to your room," said Livy. "I'll give you some plates and silverware, and you should be set to enjoy it."

"I'll donate mine to the people here," said the other guest.

"We're going to take ours home," said the man in the group, receiving a smile from his wife. "My friends are never going to believe I actually baked a cake. We'll bring the plates back, though."

"That will be fine," said Livy, realizing they'd have to order special plates for classes so students wouldn't need to return them.

Brooke helped Livy box up the two cakes for them, and when they were finally alone in the kitchen, Brooke turned to Livy. "Is there anything I can do for you? I know something's wrong. You haven't been yourself."

"Thanks for the offer, but I'll be fine. Austin and I have to work a few things out, that's all."

"Trouble in paradise?" Brooke asked, giving her a sympathetic look.

"No, not for us," Livy said. The more she'd thought about Aynsley and her claim, the more determined she'd become to stick by Austin. They'd bared their souls to one another. She wouldn't discard their relationship. That was too close to what he'd suffered from the constant seesawing of his mother's affection.

"Well, if you need any help from me, you've got it," said Brooke, giving her a quick hug.

Livy blinked away tears and hugged her back, telling herself to get better control, or the whole story would come out.

After spending time with the guests, Livy trotted to Gran's house eager to get into more comfortable clothes and have some time to herself.

She was in her room reading when her cell chimed. *Austin.* She snatched the phone and clicked on the call. "Hi, what's up?"

"Well, I've spent some time talking to Aynsley. She's

keeping to her story, and I agreed to a DNA test. I've had a swab done on my inside cheek, but it will be a couple of weeks until we have the result."

"In either case, it will be best to have the truth," said Livy, wishing she didn't feel the need to cry again.

"I think so, too," said Austin. "I spoke to her about her financial situation, and she's desperate for money. Brooke told me Aynsley was overly impressed by my money. I think she's right. Aynsley is already talking about my obligation to pay for the baby."

"It's not just your money. I've seen the way she looks at you. She's interested in you too," said Livy, forcing herself to be truthful, though she hated saying the words.

"I've told her no matter what the situation turns out to be, I'm not interested in a relationship with her. I think she finally understands," said Austin, a steely tone to his words.

"I'm here for you regardless of the outcome," Livy said, meaning it.

"Thank you. That's what's keeping me going during this nightmare."

"Has she spoken to any of your friends about the situation?" Livy asked.

"Yes. That's another issue. She's spreading the word, and there's not much I can say except I believe she's wrong. Until we have proof, what else is there?" Austin snorted with disgust. "It's so unfair. It's wrong not to be able to defend yourself by just denying it. I've talked to a lawyer friend of Shane's, and if it comes to it, he'll help me sort things out."

"I'm sorry, Austin. I really am," said Livy, wishing there was something she could do for him. They'd just have to wait for test results. If she could only hold herself together until then.

CHAPTER FIFTEEN

CHARLOTTE

"Wha-a-a-t?" Charlotte said, her pulse sprinting. "Is it true?"

Shane shook his head. "I don't think so. Aynsley is telling everyone Austin is the father, but I believe my brother when he says he's sure he's not."

"What about Livy? She must be heartbroken," said Charlotte feeling sick. "She and Austin are so happy together."

"Livy's standing by him," said Shane. "But Austin is devastated that he's hurt her."

"I feel bad for them both. Brooke told me weeks ago that she had met Aynsley and didn't like her, that she was very materialistic. Do you think she's trying to get Austin's money?"

"The thought has crossed our minds," said Shane, shaking his head sadly. "I know her ex-husband, and according to him, Aynsley's constant need for things is what drove him to make some bad decisions, and they lost most everything. At least for the time being. He comes from a wealthy family. But I'm betting there's more to it than that."

"So, there is definite motivation for her doing something like this to Austin," said Charlotte. "Is she spreading the news on social media?"

"Just among friends in Miami, I understand. But I wouldn't put it past her to go wide online. At Austin's request, I've sent her a letter warning her of consequences if she tries anything like that. He's already given a DNA sample since the pregnancy is past the seven-week point. But it could be weeks before a result comes back."

"Poor Livy," said Charlotte. "When I return to the cove, I'll try to find out what I can do to help."

"Let's hope it's the scam we think it is," said Shane grimly.

CHAPTER SIXTEEN

LIVY

Livy sat with her two cousins in the office at the Inn trying to focus on plans for an upcoming wedding. But her heart wasn't in it. How could she be excited about a wedding when her life had been torn apart by what she believed was a lie?

Austin had returned to the Gulf Coast but had more or less holed up in his beach house working on a computer project to keep busy. Livy didn't blame him. He was dealing with anger and frustration about a situation over which he had no control.

Though he warned her he wasn't pleasant company, Livy refused to allow him to wallow in self-pity and visited as often as she could. He never turned her away.

"This will be our biggest wedding yet," said Brooke. "What if the weather doesn't hold?"

They'd planned to set up a buffet in the dining room and provide seating there and out on the patio and pool deck as well.

"If it rains, in addition to using the dining room, we'll temporarily turn the breakfast area and gathering room into seating for the dinner," said Charlotte. "This client is a referral from Rosalie at Tropi-Flowers, and I promised we'd do an excellent job for them."

"We'd better alert Amby that we might need him and a helper that day," said Brooke. Ambrose Pappas was groundskeeper and all-around handyman at the Inn and had worked for Gran for years. His wife, Beryl, was head of the housekeeping staff. They were like family.

"Okay, are you all set, Livy?" Charlotte asked gently. Ever since they'd talked about the situation with Austin, Charlotte had been solicitous of her.

"I'm fine," Livy said, wishing it were true. "Plans for the wedding are all set. We've hired extra cooks for the event, and Holly has three friends helping to serve. The bartender we hired has found two waiters to handle the bars and pouring wine for dinner."

"Great," said Charlotte. "Brooke and I will handle everything else."

"Of the one hundred guests, only forty are staying here at the inn. That will be easier than having them all here." Brooke gave them a thumbs up sign. "If we can pull off this wedding, we can do anything."

"You got that right," said Charlotte. "Now, let's relax at Gran's. We have some time before we have to get ready for the social hour."

"Okay," said Brooke. "The next few days are going to be busier than ever."

Livy followed her cousins to Gran's house eager to have some time away from the Inn. She'd started a thorough cleaning of the kitchen cupboards and storage areas in anticipation of Gran and John's return. It was another way to keep her mind off Austin and Aynsley.

In her room, Livy put on her swimsuit and went to join her cousins at Gram's private pool, trying to pull herself out of a funk. While she believed Austin about the night he'd spent with Aynsley, she knew others might not. Especially with Aynsley telling their friends a different story. It rankled, but as Austin said, there wasn't much they could do about it at this point.

As she approached the pool, Charlotte called to her.

"C'mon in. The water's fine."

Brooke was sitting on the edge at the deep end of the pool dangling her feet in the water. "Come sit by me."

Livy smiled and turned to Charlotte. "I'll sit with Brooke and then come in the water with you, Charlie."

She sat next to Brooke and sighed with contentment. After standing for much of each day in the kitchen, it felt good to kick and wiggle her feet in the water.

"How're you doing, Livy?" Brooke asked, giving her a look of concern. "This is a horrible time for you."

Livy shrugged. "I'm trying not to think of Austin and what he's going through. It's tough because I thought we might begin planning for a future together."

"But you love Austin," prompted Brooke.

"Oh, yes, that won't change, but circumstances might change his thinking. That's the difficult part. This wait-and-see game is the worst. Aynsley has the power to change our lives. I believe she knows what she's saying isn't true, but she'll pursue it, hurting others in the process, including Austin and me. I just don't understand why."

"I didn't like her when I first met her. It was obvious she was interested only in Austin's money." Brooke shook her head. "Too bad we can't all speak up about it, but I think Austin is right when he says just to keep it quiet."

"Gran always said, 'The truth doesn't cost anything, but a lie could cost you everything'. Aynsley may think she's doing something to help her future, but I believe Gran. It's not going to turn out well for Aynsley no matter what she thinks."

"Time will take care of it," said Brooke. "But you can talk to me about it anytime. I know how hard this must be for you."

Charlotte joined them. "Talking about Aynsley?"

Brooke sighed. "Trying to help Livy keep her spirits up."

"Shane is furious that Aynsley would make such an

accusation about Austin. He's doing some investigation of his own." Charlotte patted Livy on the back. "Don't worry. The truth always comes out in the end."

"I know," said Livy. "That's what I have to keep remembering. But I hate to see how Aynsley is hurting Austin. It's a terrible betrayal of their friendship."

Charlotte stood. "Hate to be the nag, but it's time to get ready."

Livy went inside with her cousins and up to her room. Her phone was lying on top of the bed, and she saw she'd received a message from her mother. She opened it and after reading it plopped down on the bed feeling nauseous. The message said her mother couldn't wait to meet Austin, had already planned to have an engagement party for them, and might even come a few days early to the family reunion to spend some time with Livy planning the party.

The thought of having her mother meet Austin amidst the turmoil he was going through sent her pulse into overdrive. The last thing Austin or she needed was the appearance of her mother coming to check on them.

Livy was still sitting on the bed when Charlotte knocked on the door and opened it. "Why aren't you ready?"

Brooke joined them.

Livy held up the phone and told her about the message. "My mother is going to freak when she hears about Austin and the situation he's in. She's already planning an engagement party, and we're not even engaged."

"What!" said Charlotte, taking a seat on the bed beside her and wrapping an arm around her. "First, there's no reason she'd hear anything about it. Austin has asked everyone here at the cove not to mention the situation to anyone else, and I don't believe they will. Secondly, tell your mother you'll let her know when it's time for such a party, and until then she needs to stop."

"By the time Gran and John are back and the family party is held here, you will, I hope, have results of the DNA test," said Brooke. "This whole thing is so crazy, no one believes it anyway. Try to put aside your worries. You have a few weeks before Gran and John return."

Livy sighed. "You're right. I shouldn't be so worried, but my mother is so excited that it's going to take work to keep her in Virginia."

"One step at a time," said Charlotte. "Right now, we're going to meet and greet our guests." She studied Livy. "Why don't you skip this evening? Brooke and I will handle it, and you can visit Austin."

Livy felt a smile spread across her face. "Thanks. I made cupcakes earlier. I think I'll take some to him."

After her cousins left, she dressed for a casual evening with Austin. She decided to surprise him, hoping it would give her a better idea of how he was handling this.

She went to the Inn, slipped into the kitchen to get the cupcakes, and then headed down the coast to Austin's house.

As she pulled into Austin's driveway, Livy was surprised to see an unfamiliar car in the driveway. She thought about turning around but decided not to. Instead, she got out of the car, gathered her plate of cupcakes, and walked to the front door.

At the sound of voices inside, she called, "Hello. Austin?"

Austin appeared at the doorway looking frazzled. "Hi, Livy. What are you doing here?"

She froze. He never spoke to her like that.

"Sorry, I didn't mean that the way it sounded. Come on in. Aynsley's ex-husband is here." He held the door open and kissed her on the cheek. "See you brought some of those cupcakes of yours." Tension radiated off his body.

She stepped inside and stood facing a man of average height who was dressed in tan slacks and a navy blazer. His dark hair hung below his collar, and his brown eyes focused on her.

"This is Laurence Lynch," said Austin. "Laurence, this is Olivia Winters."

Livy bobbed her head. "Hello." She wondered why he was there but didn't ask the question or say anything else in her confusion.

"Look, I'll go now. But, Austin, I'll be in touch later. You can count on it." Laurence gave Austin a little salute and left.

After he left, Austin collapsed on the couch and held his head in his hands.

Livy set the cupcakes down on the coffee table and hurried over to him. "What is it?" She sat down beside him and placed a hand on his shoulder.

He looked up at her with such sadness that Livy's breath caught. "Laurence says if it turns out I'm the father of Aynsley's baby, I shouldn't be worried about her being able to take care of the child. He'll help."

"That's outrageous. What's going on between the two of them?" asked Livy, shaken by the idea.

"I don't know, but I don't like it. When I tried to explain that I'm certain the baby isn't mine, he brushed it off. Shane did a little investigation of his own and heard that Aynsley is trying to get more money from Laurence now that he's inherited some."

"It's all such an unbelievable situation," said Livy. "I just wish you hadn't been placed in the middle of it."

"Me, too," said Austin. He stood and pulled her up beside him. "I don't know what I'd do if you weren't beside me. Do you think Aynsley was using me to make Laurence jealous? Or something like that? It almost sounded as if Laurence wants Aynsley back."

"That's weird." He brushed a hand over his head. "It's a mixed-up mess. The only thing we can do is wait for some of this to get sorted out. Regardless, we can't afford to dwell on it. We have to move forward."

He wrapped his arms around her and placed his lips on hers for a tender kiss. When they pulled apart, he gave her a smile. "Let's try to get back to normal." He lifted the cover off the plate of cupcakes, lifted one up, and took a bite.

Grinning, Livy said, "C'mon. Let's take these into the kitchen and get something cold to drink." She decided not to say anything about her mother's message. Austin had enough to handle already.

Later, they sat on the screened-in porch and watched the sun go down.

"Another day of waiting," sighed Austin.

Livy turned to him. "We need to keep positive. As Gran always says, 'Worry is a waste of time.' Charlie and Brooke were helping me earlier with that thought. Now, I'll help you. Let's go to our favorite place and relax."

"What if one of Aynsley's friends is there?"

With more bravado than she felt, Livy shrugged. "We'll simply say hello as usual."

Austin laughed. "Okay, I can do that. You're right. Time to get out of here and stop hiding. Who knows when we'll get the results?"

"As long as it's before Gran and John return, we'll be fine," said Livy, feeling better. A night out was just what they needed.

CHAPTER SEVENTEEN

ELLIE

Ellie sat in the tasting room of a vineyard not far from Lausanne, Switzerland, thinking of Sanderling Cove and the people there. She and John had enjoyed a fantastic summer, but as the time drew near for a return to Florida, she grew more eager to get home.

Earlier, she'd read Liz's note with satisfaction.

With all three of her granddaughters prepared to go forward into the future with good men by their sides, she felt as if she'd accomplished what she'd set out to do. She glanced at John, who was busy talking with one of the owners of the vineyard about the delicious white wine they produced. He'd loved every minute of their trip.

Soon, not now, she'd encourage him to go back home a week or so early, and surprise everyone.

CHAPTER EIGHTEEN

LIVY

Livy scanned the interior of the Pink Pelican to see if any of their friends were there. Seeing none, she let out a sigh of relief and followed Austin out to the patio. At this hour they were able to find a table alongside the sand and quickly claimed it.

"Ah, this is perfect. It's important for me to get away from the Inn and for you to get out of your house. You said you've been working on a new project. Ready to tell me about it?"

He shook his head. "Not yet. Still trying to figure out if it'll work and if it's worth the effort. More importantly, I've been reaching out to other people in the field to see if anyone is interested in working on a project with me." He lifted Livy's hand. "After meeting you and living in Florida for a while, I like the idea of staying here, with breaks to visit cooler places during the summer. How does that sound?"

"Delightful," said Livy. Was he thinking of a future with her?

"I know we have to put plans on hold for now, but I'm thinking ahead," said Austin, turning as a waitress approached them.

They gave their drink orders and then stared out at the water beyond the sandy beach. Livy wasn't sure what it was about the water that soothed her, but as usual when she watched the waves roll in to kiss the shore and pull away, she felt some of the tension leave her shoulders.

The waitress returned with their drinks. They were tasting their beers when Livy looked up to see Justin and Izzy

Schuyler walk onto the patio. Izzy saw them and led Justin to their table. "Hi, you two. Mind if we join you?"

"Not at all," said Livy as Austin stood and shook hands with Justin. She'd liked Izzy and Justin when she'd met them earlier.

After they were settled at the table and had ordered their drinks, Izzy turned to Livy. "I'm very sorry about the situation with Austin," she said softly while the men chatted. "How's he doing? How are you?"

"We're pretty certain that this is an underhanded way of Aynsley trying either to get Austin's money or to get her ex back. Austin says there's no way he's the father of her child, and Aynsley knows it. We're both furious that she's doing this."

"I think she's trying to get Laurence back. He inherited a lot of money, and she has this idea of making him jealous because he's the one who wanted a family, not her." Izzy shook her head. "At this point, neither Justin nor I want anything to do with her."

"Austin and I won't relax until the DNA results come back. Then we'll have positive proof that this whole thing has been one gigantic lie." Livy took a deep breath to calm herself. "It's wrong that she can make an accusation like that, and there's little he can do about it without proof."

"Surely people who know Austin don't believe her," said Izzy with a note of disbelief. "If Austin thought the baby was his, he wouldn't claim otherwise."

"Austin and Aynsley have gone to a couple of large social events where everyone saw them together," Livy said. "So, it's kind of a 'he said, she said' deal. That's what makes it so difficult."

"I wish there was something I could do to help you," said Izzy.

"There is," said Livy plainly. "Every time you hear someone make a comment about this, set them straight."

Izzy studied her. "That won't be a problem. I've already set a few people straight."

"Thank you," Livy said quietly. "I appreciate that, and Austin would feel the same way."

Izzy squeezed her hand.

Livy took comfort from the gesture. Other people believed Austin. They knew the kind of man he was. She took another sip of her beer and turned her attention to the men's conversation.

"Livy is interested in staying in the area, so I'm trying to set up something here. We'll see," said Austin.

The four of them shared pleasant conversation over dinner, and then when the D.J. began playing some softer music, Austin asked Livy to dance. Izzy and Justin joined them on the sand, and soon, others did too.

When Livy settled in Austin's arms, all her worries were put aside as they moved in rhythm to the music. It felt so natural to be in his arms, Livy sighed. This is where she needed to be, wanted to be. Always. She thought of something going on between Austin and Aynsley, and her stomach took a dive. Maybe Austin had been too drunk to remember the next morning but not too drunk to have sex.

"Hey, what's wrong?" Austin whispered in her ear.

"Nothing," Livy replied firmly. She couldn't let her thoughts get out of control. She knew Austin for the decent man he was. She couldn't believe anything else.

She rested her head against Austin's chest and allowed the music to carry her away to a time when all would be settled, and plans for the future might include a wedding.

Back at Austin's house, they relaxed on the porch for a while, allowing the cool air to encircle them. Summers in Florida were hot and humid, but she liked nighttime hours that caressed her skin with cool kisses. Tonight of all nights this seemed so right.

Later, inside, she was just as open to Austin's kisses, and when he offered his hand to lead her into his bedroom, she didn't hesitate.

Lying beside Austin later, gazing up at the ceiling fan circling above them, Livy became determined to handle any situation that came up with Aynsley. She turned and faced Austin. In sleep, his face was relaxed, giving him a boyish look. An urge to protect him swept through her. He'd been through a lot growing up. She hoped going forward he'd know he could trust her to support him.

He stirred and opened his eyes. His lips curved and he reached out to her. "Livy, my sweet Livy."

She nestled against him, and soon they were both asleep.

When Livy walked into the Inn's kitchen the next morning, Billy Bob glanced at the clock and gave her a wink.

A flush that filled her cheeks. She supposed everyone, including the staff at the Inn, knew she and Austin were together.

Billy Bob came over to her. "It's all right, little lady. I've got things under control."

Livy gazed up at him. "I know I can count on you. Thanks. I appreciate it."

"Things a little better?" he asked, looking at her with concern.

She shrugged. "I hope so. But right now, we all need to concentrate on upcoming plans for the big wedding. Heard any weather reports lately?"

His brow creased with worry. "Yeah, and it doesn't look good. A tropical depression is headed our way."

"What? Are you kidding?" Livy's heart stopped and then her pulse raced.

"Nope," Billy Bob said. "Your cousins are already here and are in the office to discuss it."

"Will you handle the next few breakfasts while I go talk with them?" she asked.

"Sure thing," he said. "Got a few on the way right now."

"Bless you," Livy said and hurried to the office.

Charlotte and Brooke looked up when she entered the room.

"Have you heard the news?" Brooke asked, shaking her head. "I don't know what we're going to do."

"We have to make this wedding the best it can be," said Charlotte firmly, making her seem a little bit like the bossy child she could be when she was younger. Livy loved her for it.

"Since we don't want to go ahead with a beach wedding, we could aim for holding the ceremony in the gazebo," Charlotte continued. "But if the weather reports are correct, even that venue is iffy. I suggest we count on having an indoor wedding."

"But what about the bride and groom? They wanted to be on the beach or in the gazebo," Livy said.

"I have an idea." Brooke said. "It's something I saw in a bride's magazine recently. Hold on. I'll get it and be right back."

While Brooke was gone, Charlotte faced Livy. "How are things going with Austin? Shane is worried about him."

"It was the weirdest thing. When I got to his house the other day, Aynsley's ex, Laurence Lynch, was there. There's something going on with him and Aynsley. She's trying to get him back because of his recent inheritance."

"Shane doesn't speak well of either of them," said Charlotte. "Let's just hope the circumstances get resolved quickly."

"I don't want my mother to know anything about it," said Livy with feeling. "She's already planning an engagement party even though we're not engaged. And if she thinks Austin has gotten another woman pregnant, she'll have a fit."

Charlotte placed a hand on her shoulder. "We all know Austin for the fine person he is."

"Thanks. I just don't want him to get hurt even more by this mess."

Their conversation ended when Brooke burst into the room holding up a magazine. She took a seat between them and spread the magazine open on the desk. "I think this might work for us, if we can get Adam to use his time off from the construction business to help us."

A picture showed an eight-foot backdrop of white-painted wooden lattice work with narrow sides and a small roof above it.

"Rosalie could do her thing with flowers. It would have some of the same look as the gazebo, but we'd place it indoors in the dining room," Brooke said, giving them a look of triumph.

"But what about the dinner?" said Livy. "We were going to set up tables and a buffet there."

"A buffet could be set up in the breakfast room and the adjoining gathering room," said Charlotte. "If we served cocktails in the dining room following the ceremony while the buffet is being set up, we could then move people out of the dining room and have Amby and a crew set up tables there. I don't think people will mind standing around with cocktails waiting to go through the buffet. That usually happens anyway."

"Wow," said Livy. "You've really thought this through, Charlie. I'm impressed."

Charlotte laughed. "I've had plenty of time to think of this. I heard the weather report last night and didn't sleep a whole lot."

"Okay, I'll take care of Amby and getting a crew together to set up tables and move things around," said Brooke. "I can talk to Adam too to see if he'll help build our mini-gazebo."

"Tell him if he does this for us, I'll supply him with all the cookies he wants going forward," said Livy.

"How about your cupcakes?" said Brooke grinning.

"Those too," said Livy, laughing. She was glad she wasn't in this wedding business alone.

"I'll call the bride and tell her what we have in mind. Do you mind if I show her the picture you have, Brooke?"

"Not at all. I think we can pull this off to make it even better than the photograph."

"I'm going to call Rosalie first," said Charlotte, "and tell her what we have in mind. Since it's her referral to us, I want to make sure Rosalie is happy with our new plans."

"Good luck," said Brooke. "Let's meet back here in an hour with an update."

Livy left the office with her mind spinning. The menu for the group was fairly easy—a steamship round roast, poached salmon, and a selection of salads and side dishes. They'd be dished up in the kitchen and brought out to the buffet at the last minute. The cake, a chocolate with a white buttercream frosting, would be placed on display in the dining room when the time came.

She entered the kitchen and easily slipped into her role beside Billy Bob. They'd developed a pleasant relationship made closer by Billy Bob's encounter with Wayne.

"Everything okay with the wedding?" he asked her.

"I think so," she answered. "It's going to be a hectic day, but I'm sure we can pull it off."

"That's good because they're now saying it's going to be a tropical storm."

Livy met in the office with her cousins.

They faced one another with grim expressions. The weather forecast remained worrisome as they tuned into the local weather channel once more.

"The best news is that Adam says he can have a mini gazebo built that'll even be better than the photo. He'll use white latticework that is plastic coated so it can be a prop for us for the future. He'll have it done the night before, allowing Rosalie to decorate it," Brooke announced.

"I talked to Rosalie and then called Amy to talk to her about the change in venue," said Charlotte. Amy Dickson and her groom, Craig Howell, were a darling couple, both schoolteachers. Their budget was limited which was why Rosalie was donating her services for free, and the Sanderling Cove Inn was providing a free cake. Amy, the eldest of three girls in her family, had already mentioned the possibility of her youngest sister getting married at the Inn next year.

"Was Amy terribly disappointed?" asked Brooke.

Charlotte shook her head. "No, she's grateful we're thinking ahead because she was worried that they'd have to cancel the whole thing. She loved the idea of the mini gazebo look. And with her bridesmaids in turquoise, she thinks they and the colorful tropical flowers will add a brightness to the room that will outshine the storm."

Livy felt her lips curve. Amy was one of the sweetest brides they'd had. "I have things in the food department under control. But the thought of people milling around all day inside and getting in the way is scary. So, I thought of making goody bags with popcorn and other treats for everyone to take to their rooms that afternoon. We can call it a reading and movie afternoon."

"Great idea," said Brooke, clapping her hands. "I was getting worried about that. If it's just raining, most people will venture out, but with a possible storm like this they won't want to."

"Okay, we've got a plan," said Livy, relieved they could work with this. "Time for a group hug."

The three of them stood, and chuckling happily, hugged one another.

CHAPTER NINETEEN

BROOKE

Brooke was just mixing some paints in Dylan's studio when she got a call from her mother. She smiled before she even clicked on the call. She and her mother had been exchanging news about the forthcoming family party, which was scheduled for a long weekend after Gran and John returned to Sanderling Cove. This gathering would be something new for her mother because, for the first time ever, she'd be accompanied by a man. Her mother sounded like a schoolgirl when she talked about Chet Brigham, her nurse and the man she'd fallen in love with.

"Hi, Mom. What's up?"

Her mother giggled and then gave a soft sob.

Brooke's heart fell. "What's wrong? Are you okay?"

"Yes, yes," her mother got out between shaky breaths. "It's Chet. He's asked me to marry him, and I said yes."

"Oh, Mom, that's wonderful! I'm so happy for you! I can't wait to get to know him." She didn't want to confess to her mother that Chet had called her earlier to ask for Brooke's approval. It had been a heartfelt conversation that meant a lot to each of them.

"I'm thrilled," her mother said. "It's taken years, but I've finally found someone I want to spend the rest of my life with. I know you and I have always been a team, but now we're both with the men we love. But I know we'll be there for one another if needed."

"True," Brooke replied, blinking back tears. This news was the final piece of information she needed to move forward with her plans to live in two different places away from New York, where her mother lived.

"We haven't set a date, but I don't think it'll be too long before we get married," her mother said. "There's really nothing stopping us. We'll probably make it after the summer, when you and Dylan can be present."

"That'll be perfect," said Brooke. "Who would've guessed a few months ago that this would have happened to both of us."

"Some miracles just seem to pop out of thin air," said her mother. "I'm so glad for ours."

They chatted for a few more minutes, and then Brooke said goodbye. Full of joy, she did a little jig and then went back to work on the portrait she was making of her mother.

CHAPTER TWENTY

LIVY

Livy ran into the kitchen, breathless from the dash from Gran's house to the Inn with a tarp thrown over her head. As predicted, downpours and a strong breeze had arrived proving that all their changes in plans for the wedding were wise.

She was alone when she turned on the kitchen lights, sending a glow into the gloominess from outside. Today was going to be a challenge, but one they were prepared to handle.

She went into the office to check reservations. One couple had cancelled their trip from Canada with regrets but two more, part of the wedding party, had decided to stay at the Inn because they didn't want to travel in the storm that was supposed to hit later in the day. She made notes for Brooke and set them in the office chair for her to see.

Back in the kitchen, Livy pulled out muffins she'd made and frozen and set them in a warming oven. Then she made coffee and set up the sideboard in the breakfast room with a selection of juices, a plate of cookies, and the coffee service. Early risers could come for a hot drink or water and a snack before breakfast time.

She'd just finished pouring coffee into a cup for herself when Amy appeared.

"What are you doing up this early?" asked Livy. "You're supposed to be sleeping in for your big day."

Amy trailed a hand through her shoulder-length brown hair. "I couldn't sleep. Too excited. The day isn't at all what I'd planned, but thanks to quick work on your end, it's going to be the best it can be with this weather. That's what I keep telling myself."

"There's something to be said for cozy and intimate," Livy said, hoping to be upbeat.

"I guess. My hairdresser has promised to come here to fix hair for me and my sisters so we don't have to go out in the rain."

"That's nice of her," said Livy impressed. "I want to be sure to meet her so we can suggest her for other brides."

"That would be great. She's a family friend." Amy poured herself a cup of coffee and turned to her. "I'm glad we didn't try to have a wedding at my parent's house like Craig and I originally talked about."

"I think you'll be pleased. A lot of people are working hard to make this satisfying for you," Livy said with pride.

"Thank you," said Amy. "See you later."

After she left, Livy hurried into the kitchen. There was a lot to do.

Later that morning, Livy walked into the dining room to see what Rosalie was doing with the flowers.

Charlotte and Brooke were already there standing aside as Rosalie stood on a ladder and wove flowers into the design of the lattice work.

Livy's breath caught at the beauty of it. The effect was of a living garden behind the small table that would be placed for the minister to use.

"This is even better than we imagined," said Brooke. "The colors are outstanding."

Charlotte nudged Brooke. "You and your colors."

Brooke laughed. "I can't help it. Now that I can see them so clearly, it's opened up a whole new world for me."

With Dylan's encouragement, the artistic talent Brooke had kept hidden behind her practical job had emerged.

Feeling that things were in good hands, Livy returned to the kitchen to finish icing the cake and to start prepping salads and sides. She sometimes felt like an orchestra leader coordinating the timing of everything, allowing all the offerings to be served together.

Austin entered the kitchen.

She grinned as he approached her and gave her a kiss on the cheek. "Hi, Chef. I'm to report to duty in the dining room to help move stuff around. Will you have time for a break later on?"

"I don't know," she answered with a teasing smile. "But I'll try."

He laughed and headed out to the dining room. She watched him go, liking the view.

Aware Billy Bob and the other kitchen helpers were watching, she chuckled. She didn't care who knew how she felt about Austin.

###

When it came time for the ceremony, Livy joined her cousins and other staff members to watch from the back of the room. She'd found something special from each wedding they'd coordinated. Even from the one where the groom took off before the ceremony. She knew from her meetings with both Amy and Craig that this was going to be special.

Craig stood beside the minister with his brother as best man. At the sound of Wagner's Bridal Chorus, the music known as *Here Comes the Bride*, people sitting in the chairs on either side of the aisle rose to their feet.

Amy's sisters, one blonde and the other with brown hair, entered the room and made their way down the aisle. Their simple, sleeveless turquoise dresses were perfect on this stormy day. Their bright-colored bouquets added a festive note. And when Amy appeared wearing a tea-length white-lace dress, several gasps of delight echoed throughout the room. The scoop-necked bodice was decorated with small white pearls. A single drop pearl hung from the silver necklace she wore around her neck and matched the earrings that were displayed with Amy's brown hair pulled back from her face. A shimmering smile crossed Amy's lovely face as tears of joy filled her eyes, touching Livy's heartstrings. The hush in the room told Livy she wasn't the only one who felt that way.

Livy's gaze turned to Craig. His eyes remained focused on Amy, welling with tears of his own.

Beside her, Amy's father was openly crying. Her mother, sitting in the front row dabbed at her eyes. After surviving many personal challenges, this couple was the one everyone wanted to see married.

The ceremony began and the room was totally silent as people leaned forward to hear the exchange of vows. Short, simple, but meaningful words of dedication.

Livy, like others around her, sighed after the minister pronounced them man and wife, and Amy and Craig kissed.

Austin stepped behind her and placed a hand on her shoulder. "Pretty special, huh?"

She nodded. "Are you here to help?"

He gave her a little salute. "Yep. I'm following orders. I'm to move chairs and set up tables as quickly as possible."

They moved aside as people left the dining room and headed to the bar in the gathering room.

"I've got to go to the kitchen. See you later." Livy turned to go but was held back.

She looked up at Austin as he bent to kiss her.

"M-m-m," he whispered. "Until then."

Enjoying the feel of his lips on hers, she forced herself to pull away. "Later."

He grinned. "That a promise?"

"You bet," she said before hurrying away.

After the last of the dishes had been carried into the kitchen and the men were busy breaking down the tables in the dining room and putting chairs into the storeroom, Livy stood with her cousins at the kitchen counter. The two dishwashers were running, and the pots and pans were being handwashed by the staff.

"We did it," said Brooke. She walked over to the kitchen table and took a seat. Livy and Charlotte joined her. It would be a while before the last wedding guest went to bed, but a sense of accomplishment filled Livy. The storm that had raged most of the day seemed to be winding down, and soon this whole, exhausting day would become a memory for them to share.

"Even those wedding guests who aren't staying at the Inn are hanging around. I overheard a couple of them talking about how the Inn was a perfect venue for weddings, almost as if one were opening a lovely home to them," said Charlotte. "That's an idea we can work on for the website and in our PR strategy."

"I think so too. But we need to be as well prepared for another group as large as this." Brooke turned to Livy. "Isn't your friend's cousin planning to have about one hundred people?"

"Oh, you mean SueEllen's cousin. That's the last I heard," Livy said. "But it's not for several months. Thank heaven. With all that's going on with me and Austin, the idea of facing anyone from home is downright frightening."

"By then, the Inn should be much more able to handle

weddings of that size, unless Gran and John don't want to do that anymore," said Charlotte.

"Not even with our help?" Livy said, dismayed. She'd grown to love working with weddings.

"It's all sort of a waiting game right now," Charlotte said. "There's so much we don't know about the future."

Livy swallowed hard, trying not to think of Aynsley.

As if her thoughts had conjured him up, Austin appeared with Shane and Dylan.

"Sitting down on the job?" Dylan asked with a teasing grin.

"Just taking a break," said Brooke. "Thank you, guys, for helping."

"Yes, we really appreciate it," added Charlotte.

Austin placed a hand on Livy's shoulder. "Glad we could help."

She patted his hand wishing this romantic wedding hadn't caused her worries to grow about their uncertain future.

Livy and her cousins made sure the night manager was settled and then headed over to Gran's house.

In the kitchen, Shane, Dylan, and Austin were sitting at the table eating pizza and sipping beer.

"Thought you women might be hungry," said Shane.

Livy laughed with the others. They'd been preparing food all day. Still, the smell of garlic and tomatoes made her mouth water. Surprising how much appetite she'd built while working.

"Smells delicious," said Charlotte, pulling up a chair and moving so Livy could sit in the chair next to Austin.

Brooke handed Charlotte and Livy plates loaded with a slice of margherita pizza.

"I'll get you some beer," said Dylan jumping to his feet.

When they were all gathered around the table, it was quiet for a moment as they ate, and then they all began to talk about the day.

"I think we've hit a milestone," said Brooke. "The wedding of one hundred did just fine, but more than that will be a problem. But we've been thinking of smaller weddings when we could make more money with larger weddings."

"But we had to hire more staff," said Livy. She sent the men a teasing smile. "Though some of our labor was free."

"We'll see about that," said Shane, wiggling his eyebrows at Charlotte, and they all laughed.

It was a congenial group. Livy especially liked the fact that all the men got along despite their differences. Her thoughts flew to Gran. Did she suspect this is how the summer would go? She and the other grandmothers sure were happy about the way things were turning out. If Livy only knew what the future held for her.

CHAPTER TWENTY-ONE

LIVY

Several days later, Livy woke up in her bedroom frustrated and angry that her future with Austin had been jeopardized by a hideous accusation. What should've been a time of happiness between them had turned into a push-pull situation between contentment and frustration. This emotional tug of war was, she realized, pretty much like a lot of Austin's childhood and his relationship with his mother.

She checked her bedside clock. It was still early.

Livy climbed out of bed, pulled on a pair of shorts and a T-shirt and headed out to the beach. She needed the comfort of the waves, the cries of the birds to settle her emotions. If she were lucky, she wouldn't bump into anyone she knew. She needed to do some real soul searching. Livy slipped out of the house grateful no one else was awake to see her leave.

The sun was still deciding whether to show a bright face or hide behind some low-lying clouds. She headed straight for the water's edge. She needed the waves' salty kisses at her ankles to give her a better outlook on life.

She stepped into the frothy edges of the water and sighed with contentment. The waves rushing in and pulling away in a rhythm as old as time always humbled her. They, like the stars in the sky at night, made her realize that she was but one creature in the world with an opportunity to be her best.

All the emotions of the past couple of weeks ripped through her with painful images and memories. Time to let them go, she told herself, and took a deep breath.

One of the guests from the Inn walked onto the beach holding a net bag for storing shells. Livy returned her smile and walked in the opposite direction.

As the sun's rays brightened the sand in front of her, Livy longed for the time when her worries would be over. For now, she'd do as Austin had asked, and give him some time alone.

She was walking back to Gran's house when a small figure came running up to her. "Hi, Livy."

Livy held out her arms. Skye jumped up into them. "Daddy says I can play with Sari today."

"How wonderful. I know she's your best friend."

'Uh, huh. Daddy's best friend is Miss Madison, my teacher," said Skye.

Livy couldn't help the smile that spread across her face. They were a great couple, a delightful family together.

She set Skye down as Adam approached. "You're up earlier than usual."

"I had a lot to think about," Livy admitted. "I want to thank you again for putting together the mini gazebo for the wedding last week. It worked out perfectly."

Adam bobbed his head. "Happy to help. It was quite a storm. Hope it isn't an early sign of our hurricane season."

"Me, too." She gave him a little wave. "I'd better go. Billy Bob will beat me to the kitchen if I'm not quick enough."

They shared a laugh. Everyone at the cove had heard the news about how protective Billy Bob had been of Livy when her ex-boyfriend had confronted her. He obviously adored her.

That morning, breakfast was busy. At the last minute, the Inn had sold a lot of rooms to locals who wanted a final break before school started and fall approached. Livy was busy cleaning cupboards in preparation for John's return when she heard a familiar voice say, "Hi, Livy. Surprise!"

Gripping the edge of a shelf, Livy turned to see her mother smiling up at her.

"Hi, Mom. What are you doing here?" Livy asked, her heart pounding with distress.

"Come down here and give me a hug, sweetie pie. I'm here because I wanted to meet this handsome man of yours."

Livy swallowed hard. "Actually, we're taking some time apart." She got off the ladder and hugged her mother, remembering how her comforting embrace had always made a scraped knee or hurt feelings seem better.

"What's going on?" her mother asked, giving her a look of concern.

"It's complicated," said Livy. Her mother would be horrified to know about Aynsley's accusation.

"Well, can you stop working and fix me a cup of coffee? I could use one. Traveling isn't easy. Not even the short trip from Virginia."

"Sure, come into the breakfast room. We keep hot and cold drinks and snacks out for our guests. And then I can show you around." Grateful for the change in topic, Livy led her mother into the dining area.

Her mother gazed around. "My! Everything looks so nice. I haven't seen it in some time, but the Inn looks much more inviting. There's even a new road sign."

"Charlie, Brooke, and I have been working hard, and it's improving the Inn's image. Gran and John were in desperate need of a break. That gave us the chance to make a few changes."

Brooke walked into the room. "I thought I heard voices. Auntie Leigh, is that you?"

Livy's mother beamed at Brooke. "It is, and my, Brookie!

You look terrific. A woman in love, huh?"

Brooke embraced Leigh and grinned. "Dylan and I just fit together. You know? I can't believe how lucky I am."

"I'm happy for you. And your mother, too. I've heard she's in love."

Brooke felt her smile grow larger. "In love and engaged. I'm not sure when a wedding will take place or where. But I'm thrilled for her."

"Me, too," said Leigh. "Jo was always very devoted to you and the memory of Curt. I'm glad to see she's finally found a new love."

"How long do you plan to stay?" Brooke asked, glancing at Livy.

"I'm here for only a couple of days. I'm in charge of a social event at our golf club, but I couldn't stand being away from Livy after hearing her happy news."

"Her happy news?" said Brooke, looking confused.

"I told her I've fallen for Austin," prompted Livy.

"Oh, yes, Livy and Austin are terrific together," said Brooke beaming at her.

Leigh clasped her hands together. "I'm here to meet him. I want to get to know my future son-in-law. I'm already planning a party for the two of them at home."

Livy held up a hand to stop her. "Please don't go there. Mom, we're not even engaged."

"That may be so, but I know this time your relationship is real. You've never told me you were in love before."

"One step at a time," said Livy, trying to control the feeling of wanting to both laugh and cry.

"I'll see you two later," said Brooke. "I'm working on something in the office, and then Dylan and I are going to lunch." She gave Livy an apologetic look and left.

"I can't believe how much Brooke has changed," bubbled

her mother enthusiastically. "Is Charlie the same reserved young woman I knew?"

"She and Shane, Austin's brother, are engaged and have bought a house together in Miami. Shane's law firm is there, and Charlie is setting up her own PR business."

"So many changes this summer at the cove. You know, your grandmother and her friends were right to bring all you young people together," her mother said, brushing back a curl from Livy's cheek. "Let me know when I can meet your young man. I leave tomorrow night to get back to Virginia, and then, of course, I'll be back with Jack and the boys for the family weekend this fall."

"Okay," said Livy, wondering if Austin would be willing to help her out after requesting some time alone.

They got their coffee and treats and returned to the kitchen where they'd have privacy.

"Maribelle Sutton is dying to have me take a lot of pictures of you and Austin together. You know she's always been a little jealous of your accomplishments," said Leigh taking a seat at the table.

"Mom, I'm not competing with SueEllen on this or anything else," said Livy firmly. "After all these years, I'd think the two of you would've stopped."

Leigh sighed. "I suppose you're right, but it's almost impossible not to react. Maribelle's niece has planned a wedding here next winter all because of your job here at the Inn with your cousins."

"You know MaryBeth is going to be difficult, but there was no way I could tell her not to plan her event here," said Livy.

Her mother sighed. "Time will take care of things. You mentioned you were going to stay here in Florida. Are you going to be living with Austin? Staying here at the Inn? What?"

Livy shook her head. "Mom, there's no need to rush. There is a lot we need to discuss and decide. Until then, we plan to enjoy each other's company. That's all I can say, right now. I wish you'd talked to me before making the trip down here."

"I love surprises," said Leigh. "Aren't you glad to see me?"

"Of course, I'm glad to see you. I'm just caught off guard, that's all."

"Are you going to be able to spend the afternoon with me? I thought we could hang out at the beach or at Gran's pool."

"Sure, I can have some time with you. Have you moved into the guest room at Gran's?"

"Yes." She sighed. "It's nice to get away for even a couple of days."

"Let me finish up here, and I'll meet you at Gran's house," said Livy. "Charlie and Shane are away for the day, but we all try to be together for social time with our guests. You should see them then."

"Okay," her mother said. "I'll take my cup of coffee with me and meet you at Gran's." She stood and drew Livy up into her embrace. "I'm happy for you, honey pie. After the way your relationship with Wayne ended so abruptly, you deserve better."

If you only knew. Livy hadn't told her mother the true story about Wayne and didn't feel the need to do that right now.

Livy watched her mother leave, and as soon as she felt sure she was well on her way, she ran to get her cell phone. She punched in Austin's number and waited for him to pick up. It rang and rang and then his voice message came on.

"Austin, this is Livy. Please call me right away. My mother surprised me with a visit, and she's anxious to meet you. She knows nothing about the situation with Aynsley. Thanks."

Livy went back to cleaning the cupboard keeping one ear listening for Austin's distinctive ring tone. When she could no longer avoid going to Gran's house, she picked up her silent phone and headed there.

At the house, her mother was in a chaise lounge by the pool. "Hi, honey," she said. "Get your work done?"

"Just for today," said Livy taking a seat in a chair beside her. "I want the kitchen to be in excellent shape when John gets back."

"Is that big ex-con still working with John?" asked Leigh.

"Do you mean Billy Bob?"

"Yes," said Leigh. "That's who I meant."

"Billy Bob is a good man," gushed Livy. "I was afraid of him at first, but I've discovered he's a gentle giant."

"I'm glad to hear that. Are you happy working at the Inn?" Her mother gave her a steady look.

"Yes and no," said Livy. "I'm still questioning what I want to do after Gran and John return. But I do know I'm going to stay in Florida."

"I miss having you close by, but I understand. Right now, I'm just thinking ahead to when you get married, nothing beyond that."

Livy started to speak and then stopped. She had no idea what she could say. Austin hadn't returned her call. She got to her feet.

"I'll go change into a bathing suit and meet you down here. I'll put together a lunch for us too."

"I love that you're handy in the kitchen," said her mother, "but remember I have an important social event coming up and want to look my best, so nothing fattening."

Livy forced a smile. Her mother had always been that way, and while it meant her mother remained thin, it weirdly made Livy think she, herself, was fat.

Upstairs in her room, she tried Austin's number again and was once more sent to voice mail. If she didn't hear soon, she'd try to find some way to go to his house. Having to wait for his call was filling her stomach with acid.

After changing, she went downstairs to the kitchen and put together small salads for them to eat, using a simple oil and vinegar dressing.

She carried the food out to the patio, sat at the table with her mother, and forced herself to eat.

Her cell rang. *Austin.*

Livy grabbed it, jumped up from her chair, and hurried into the house.

"Austin, I'm glad you called. As I said, my mother is here and wants to meet you."

"Livy, I would've called earlier but I'm with Aynsley in Miami. She called last night. She's in the hospital. I'm pretty sure she's lost the baby."

"What? What does that mean?" said Livy feeling both sorrow and relief.

"Well, it doesn't mean our worries are over. We still have to face the DNA test. Funny, though, Aynsley is telling me not to worry about it."

"How long are you going to stay?"

"Not long. Laurence is arriving soon. As soon as he appears, I'm heading back to the cove. You say your mother is here?"

"Yes. She wants to meet you. I'm sorry. I know this isn't the best time ..."

"I'll be happy to meet her," said Austin. "But there's something going on with Aynsley, and I need to get to the bottom of it."

"I understand," said Livy, feeling a lump in her throat. "Can you join us for dinner?"

"Sure," said Austin. "But I won't stay long. I've been up most of the night."

"I won't mention that, but I'll think of something," said Livy. "Thanks."

"You're welcome. We'll both be on edge until we can put this mess behind us. See you later tonight."

"Or join us earlier if you wish," said Livy. She hesitated, then blurted, "My mother is a bit overeager about us being together."

"We'll deal with it," said Austin. "Glad you called."

"I love you, Austin," Livy said.

"Me, too," he said, sounding exhausted.

Livy ended the call and sighed.

CHAPTER TWENTY-TWO

LIVY

Late that afternoon, while her mother made the rounds visiting with the other cove families, Livy drove to Austin's house to make sure he was all right. She'd been worried about him driving while he was very tired but understood his need to get home.

His car was in the driveway when she pulled up to the front of his house. Relieved, she got out of the car and went to the front door. She knocked quietly, unwilling to disturb him if he was asleep.

When he didn't respond, she turned the knob. Unlocked. She opened the door and went inside. Austin was stretched out on the couch sound asleep.

She walked over and stood looking down at him. Smudges of dark color appeared beneath his eyes. She realized what a stressful time he'd just been through and reached out and caressed his cheek.

He slowly blinked his eyes open. "Hey," he murmured.

"Go back to sleep. I had to make sure you were all right."

He took hold of her hand and pulled her down beside him. "Now that you're here, I feel better."

"How was Aynsley? She must be crushed about the baby."

His features drooped. "She was. It was sad. She kept telling me she was sorry."

"I'm sorry too," Livy said. A friend of hers had miscarried and felt the emotional devastation from that loss.

"Even though I'm sure the baby wasn't mine, when Aynsley called me to come, I couldn't refuse," said Austin, looking up at her, sadness swimming in his expression.

"Of course not," Livy said, squeezing his hand.

"I need to have the results of the test before I can put this whole episode behind me," said Austin.

"I understand," Livy said. "I'm going back to the cove. I need to spend time with my mother. She wants to take us to dinner at Gavin's at the Salty Key Inn. Are you up for it?"

"I won't make it earlier, but I'll be ready for dinner. I know how much this means to you."

Livy blinked back tears and bent down to kiss him.

He put his arms around her and pulled her close. "See you tonight," he murmured before kissing her.

Feeling fresh sorrow for all that had happened, she straightened and left. She'd made a promise to support him, and she would.

That evening, Austin appeared at the Inn. Livy went right over and gave him a hug. "Thank you for coming."

He smiled at her, and when she saw the hint of his dimple beside his chin, her heart filled with love for him.

Brooke and Charlotte joined them. They knew about Aynsley's miscarriage and wanted to show their support.

"I see I'm going to have to compete to say hello," said Livy's mom joining them with a smile.

Austin held out his hand to her. "Hi, Mrs. Winters, it's nice to see you. It's been a few years."

She shook it. "Yes, and you've grown into a handsome man. In fact, you look a little like Henry, though not as much as Shane, as I remember."

"What do you think of the Inn?" he asked her. "Haven't Livy, Charlie, and Brooke done a superb job of sprucing it up a bit?"

"They used to call themselves the three musketeers," said Livy's mother. "I'm not at all surprised to see how well they're doing with it. They're quite a trio, who've always worked well together." She smiled at them. "I've had the chance to visit with the other families here at the cove, and it seems all of you grandkids have done well for yourselves. It's fantastic."

After they talked for a few minutes, Brooke and Charlotte said their farewells and left.

"We have dinner reservations for eight," said Livy's mother. "Perhaps we'd better think of leaving."

Livy gave Austin a questioning look. He still appeared to be exhausted.

He gave her a game smile. "Okay. Gavin's is my favorite restaurant here on the Gulf Coast."

"I haven't been in some time, but I can't wait to go back there," Livy's mother said.

"Well, then, let's do it," said Livy. She knew how tired Austin was and didn't want to make a long evening of it.

Gavin's was a favorite upscale restaurant of many people along the Gulf Coast and with good reason. Their food was excellent, the setting both elegant and relaxing, and the story behind it fascinating.

Now, as the hostess led them to a table along the outside wall overlooking a small garden, Livy admired the dark paneling offset by crystal sconces that shimmered like diamonds in the soft overhead light.

After they were seated, Livy's mother sighed. "Just as pretty as I remembered it. The three sisters who turned this property into a gem deserve a lot of credit. It's like you and your cousins, Livy. A real success."

"Thanks, Mom," said Livy, pleased. "I think Gran and John

are going to be pleasantly surprised."

"It will be wonderful to have everyone settled by the time the family gathering happens." Her mother beamed at Austin. "Brooke tells me she and Dylan have pretty much decided to split their time between Florida and Santa Fe. And Charlotte is happily opening her own consulting business."

His lips curved. "Yeah, it's been a great summer for everyone."

"So, when did you two start dating?" Livy's mother asked, smiling at them.

Livy cringed at the questioning but gamely answered, "We went out on a few dates just as friends, but the more time we spent together, the more our feelings grew." She glanced at Austin and back to her mother. "I had a teenage crush on him, remember?"

"Yes, I do," her mother answered, her eyes sparkling at the memory.

"And I've always liked the cookies and cupcakes she bakes," added Austin, bringing laughter to all of them.

A waiter approached them. "May I bring you sparkling water? A wine list?"

"Austin, why don't you do the honors in choosing the wine," said Leigh. She turned to the waiter, "Sparkling water would be lovely."

While Austin dealt with the wine steward about a selection, Livy's mother turned to her. "Austin was such a cute little boy. He's certainly turned into a handsome man."

"Such a great guy," said Livy.

The wine steward left, and Austin addressed them. "I've ordered a glass of champagne before dinner and depending upon what you ladies choose for your main course, we'll order something different for the meal."

"Perfect," said Livy's mother. "Being back in Sanderling

Cove and meeting you is an exciting reason to celebrate with a champagne toast."

The wine steward returned to the table with three tulip glasses and a green bottle of wine nestled in an ice bucket. After showing the bottle to Austin, he uncorked it with a soft pop, and poured some for Austin to taste. With Austin's approval, the steward poured champagne in all three flutes making sure the portions were equal.

Livy's mother lifted her glass. "Here's to the two of you and a bright future together."

Austin winked at Livy and raised his.

Livy, loving him for his kindness, raised hers in a toast she hoped would come to fruition. She knew Austin loved her, but she also was aware of how shaken he was by Aynsley's accusation and then her miscarriage.

They each ordered the special—Barramundi Fillets with Roasted Sweet Potatoes and Brussels Sprout Chips. Austin chose a bottle of Gamay Noir wine suggested by the wine steward to accompany it. Similar to a light pinot noir, Livy thought it was tasty. She liked how Austin was willing to try new things. For a foodie like her, it was important.

Conversation remained light and pleasant while they ate, centering around Austin's business and goings-on at the Inn. Livy told her mother about Grace's restaurant and how she might get into doing some specialty catering work instead of owning a bakery.

"I would think that would be a lot easier, less time-consuming," her mother agreed. "I suspect owning the bakery put a strain on your relationship with Wayne."

"That bastard!" sputtered Austin, surprising both Livy and her mother.

"Why would you say something like that?" Clearly shocked, Livy's mother's jaw dropped.

"Because he's a pig," interjected Livy. "We'll talk about it later. I don't want to ruin my meal."

Livy's mother frowned. "Oh ... kay. Obviously, I'm missing a story."

Austin reached over and squeezed Livy's hand. "You knew this time was coming."

Livy grimaced. It was time her mother knew. But she'd need to be alone with her when she told her.

The waiter cleared their plates and handed out dessert menus.

"Anyone interested in dessert?" her mother asked.

"Sure," said Austin.

"Me, too," Livy said. "I'm always curious to see what restaurants serve."

Austin settled on a decadent chocolate layer cake with layers of crème de coca-infused chocolate mousse and raspberries.

Livy chose a salted caramel apple pie. Her mother had just plain black coffee, but accepted a bite of the pie from Livy.

"Your apple pie is just as tasty," her mother commented loyally, sending smiles to Livy's face and Austin's.

Later, as they left the restaurant, they paused a moment to observe the peacock strutting across the grass in the distance. "I can't wait to come back here," said Livy.

"Maybe for another occasion," said her mother. "Maybe during our family reunion."

Austin drove them back to the cove. He climbed out of the car to thank Livy's mother's and gave Livy a quick kiss before driving off.

"I'm glad I got to know Austin a bit," her mother said, looping an arm around Livy.

"Me, too. He's had some personal issues to take care of, which is why he couldn't stay," said Livy, not about to tell her their problems. Especially because it was time to tell her about Wayne.

"Let's go inside, get comfortable, and meet on the porch," her mother suggested.

"Okay," said Livy, her stomach twisting. She wished she hadn't taken that last bite of pie because the thought of having to describe her night with Wayne was nauseating.

Later, sitting on the porch with her mother, Livy faced her and drew a deep breath.

"All right, what's all this business about Wayne?" her mother asked gently. "Austin obviously doesn't like him. What happened? Did you know he came to see me after you left for Florida?"

"No, I didn't. But I don't think he'll try that again." Livy's voice trembled. "Wayne tried to rape me. It's taken me several months to deal with that traumatic experience."

"Wha-a-a-t! He did what?" Livy's mother sat up and stared at her wide-eyed, her fists clenched.

"He ... he ... tried ...it was awful ... he pinned me down." Livy's eyes filled and overflowed as a sob escaped her. "I was so scared."

Her mother pulled Livy close and hugged her tightly. "I'm so sorry. Why didn't you tell me about Wayne?"

Livy sniffled. "I was too confused, so ashamed, I wasn't ready to tell anyone about it until one day I couldn't hold back. Austin listened to my story and was furious at Wayne for trying that. He helped me understand I had nothing to be ashamed of. It wasn't my fault. No one deserves to be treated like that."

Her mother rubbed circles on her back. "Oh, honey. I'm devastated you were treated that way. Austin is right. It's a despicable act. I thought he was a decent man." Her voice changed, became rough with anger. "If I had known what he did, I swear I would've attacked him myself."

"He's a pig," said Livy, lifting her tear-streaked face. "It's taken me awhile to understand that. I needed to rediscover not all men are like that. Austin has been very patient and encouraging me to process what happened. I will always be grateful to him for that."

"Austin is a special man," Livy's mother said, tears rolling down her cheeks.

"He found an excellent psychologist here, one he uses, to help me work through it." Livy drew in a shuddering breath and let out a long sigh. "Oh, Mom, Austin is much more than a man I'm dating. He's my everything."

"That makes me happy. I understand Austin and Shane have had a difficult time of it with their mother's overdose. I hope to be able to have the opportunity to talk to Austin again tomorrow I certainly want to thank him for his support of you."

"That would be great. But he may have to go back to Miami tomorrow." Livy didn't want to make any commitment for him. He'd done a remarkable job of being social tonight, but she knew he needed time to himself.

Her mother thumbed the tears off Livy's cheek and kissed her. "I love you, honey, more than you know. I want to assure you that you can talk to me about anything."

"I know, Mom. Thanks. Love you too," Livy replied, knowing Austin's story wasn't hers to tell.

CHAPTER TWENTY-THREE

CHARLOTTE

Charlotte watched Livy and her mother walk along the beach together. Perhaps, over the family reunion weekend, she and her mother could spend some time together. Charlotte wanted her mother to get to know Shane. One thing the summer at the cove had taught her was the importance of family. Shane's family had accepted her quickly and warmly. She'd always be grateful to them.

"Hi, Charlie," said Livy coming up to where Charlotte was standing. "Out shelling this morning?"

Charlotte shook her head. "Just enjoying the early morning coolness. It's going to be another hot day."

"You look so much like your mother, Charlotte," said Livy's mother. "She was the beautiful one of the three of us sisters."

"Yes, but you, Aunt Leigh, and Aunt Jo are pretty too," said Charlotte, twisting her long auburn hair behind her head and letting it fall to her shoulders again.

"That's lovely of you to say," said Livy's mother with a pleased smile. "It'll be fun for us all to be together. I'm happy that Jo will have an escort this time."

"More than an escort, a fiancé," Livy reminded her.

"Were you disappointed that Gran and John got married without us?" Charlotte asked Aunt Leigh.

"I was disappointed at first," said Aunt Leigh, "and then realized it was just a formality. For all intents and purposes, they were already married."

"My mother wants me to have a big, formal wedding in New York City," said Charlotte. "But that's not what I want."

"I understand, but it's a mother's wish to see her daughter married in style, wouldn't you agree?" said Aunt Leigh.

"I'll answer that," said Livy, aware the same dilemma would occur to her if she and Austin got married. "I believe each couple should decide how, when, and where they should be married. It's such a personal choice and a day never to be repeated, we hope."

Charlotte laughed and placed an arm across Livy's shoulder. "Well said, Livy. I agree with everything you mentioned."

Livy's mother shrugged and held out her arms in defeat. "Guess you two have it all figured out. What about Brooke?"

"I've heard her talk about a destination wedding in Santa Fe," said Charlotte. "We'll see." She gave Livy's mother a quick kiss on the cheek. "It's nice you're here. Have a safe flight back home tonight. And good luck with your party."

Aunt Leigh laughed. "I can see that I've missed out on a lot by staying away, but I'm happy for everyone here. It's been a beneficial summer."

"Yes," Charlotte agreed, waving at them before jogging away.

CHAPTER TWENTY-FOUR

LIVY

Livy turned to her mother. "Shall we go to Gracie's for breakfast? That's always a treat."

Her mother hesitated. "If you don't mind, I'd rather sit by Gran's pool and have a cup of coffee and, as a special splurge, one of your cupcakes."

Pleased, Livy said, "Delightful. Go ahead. I'll check in with Billy Bob and bring you cupcakes. The coffeemaker at Gran's is easy and ready to go."

"Okay, sweetheart. After hearing the horrible story about Wayne, I just want to spend as much time with you as possible." She kissed Livy's cheek. "I love you so much, and I'll always be grateful to Austin for helping you through a difficult time."

"Me, too," said Livy. "That's why I don't want to push him into anything. If the time comes when he asks me to marry him, I'll be ready. But neither of us should push him." Livy's voice held a gentle warning.

Her mother said quietly, "Yes, I understand that."

"Thanks." Livy looped a hand around her mother's arm as they left the beach.

Later, Livy joined her mother by the pool, happy to be together. She'd come to understand that though her mother sometimes seemed distracted, and her brothers competed with her for her mother's attention, love and support was there for all of them. Her mother's reaction to the news about Wayne was a perfect reminder that she cared.

After a while, she took a moment to go to her bedroom and call Austin. He picked up right away.

"Hi, Livy. What's up?"

"I was wondering if you wanted to join my mother and me for lunch at Gran's house," she said.

"I'm sorry, I can't. I've got a call into Shane and another into a man I'm thinking of doing a project with."

"Okay, I understand," said Livy. "I'll be driving my mother to the airport this evening around five o'clock. If you get a chance to say goodbye to her that would be greatly appreciated."

"I'll try," said Austin. "I really like your mother. Were you able to tell her about Wayne?"

"Yes," said Livy. "I think I've made great strides in dealing with the issue. I told her all about your help, and I know she wants to thank you for that."

"Okay, then I'll see you later."

Livy spoke softly. "Love you."

"Me, too," said Austin, leaving Livy feeling a little unsettled. Maybe it was her imagination, but he seemed a little more distant.

Warning herself not to get trapped by insecurity into creating ideas that might not be true, she headed back to the pool and her mother. Austin, the poor guy, had a lot on his plate.

Livy was delighted that both Brooke and Charlotte agreed to join her mother and her for lunch. It was a simple affair with salads, iced tea, and cookies for dessert. Sitting around the kitchen table at Gran's house, conversation flowed, stopping for a few laughs now and then, as they recalled family stories about Gran and John.

"My mother has always done things her way," said Livy's mother. "Sometimes her actions were embarrassing to me as a teenager, but Mom has a way of making people understand the amazing person she is."

"You're quite different from Gran, but you've made your mark in your community," said Livy. "That counts for a lot."

"Thanks, honey, for saying that. You've never been interested in following in my footsteps, but I care what you think about me."

Livy shrugged. "It's just a difference of opinion as to what we each want out of life."

"Talking about that," said Brooke. "How was it with you and your sisters growing up, Aunt Leigh? The three of you are very different."

Livy's mother sighed. "There was no question about that. I was the youngest and more easygoing than both Charlie's mom or your mother, Brooke. Vanessa was the oldest and wanted to do everything right. She was shattered by little Ricky's death. After her divorce, she was determined to have a strong marriage. I'm sure you, Charlotte, would agree."

"And how," said Charlie.

Her mother continued. "Jo was the romantic middle-sister who suffered headaches and depression, even as a teenager. Gran was always busy running the Inn, so we weren't as close a family as some." She held up her hand. "Not that I blame her. But to see you three girls this tight is a blessing."

Livy glanced at Charlotte and Brooke. They were more like sisters than cousins. Her mother was right. It was a true blessing.

After everyone had eaten and dishes were cleaned up, Charlotte and Brooke departed, leaving Livy alone with her mother.

"Do we have time to go shopping?" her mother asked.

"Sure, as long as it's local. We're leaving for the airport at five o'clock. Austin is going to come see you before you leave."

"The shop I want to go to isn't far. I just want a sundress. I have a couple of social events coming up, and it would be nice to have something new to wear," her mother said.

"Okay, we can do that. By the way, Mom, I appreciate your not making a big deal out of our wanting different lifestyles in our discussion at lunch."

Her mother hugged her. "Oh, honey, none of that matters after learning what happened to you and what kind of a healing summer you've been having here. I'll respect your wishes not to rush things, but when the time comes to celebrate, I hope you'll let me be part of it."

"I will, but I can't even think of that now," said Livy honestly.

"Now that that's settled, let's go shopping," said her mother.

Relieved to end the conversation, Livy got ready to leave. Shopping was an easy way to prevent any questions about Austin and the relationship she shared with him.

Two hours later, Livy and her mother returned to Gran's house and unloaded packages from her car. The end-of-summer sales had provided them both with irresistible bargains. Livy had even bought a dressy outfit that she could wear in Miami if Austin asked her to any event there.

They'd just finished carrying in their purchases when Austin arrived.

"I see you've been shopping," he said when he entered the house.

Livy's mother replied, "We got some amazing buys. I'm repacking now. Then I hope we can sit for a moment before we take off."

Austin's gaze turned to Livy. "Sorry I couldn't make it earlier."

"It's okay. We understand," she said, noting the line of worry crossing his forehead. "Let's go out to the porch. My mother can join us there."

Livy led Austin to the outside porch, eager to find out what was going on. Before she could ask him, Austin said, "I got the strangest call from Aynsley. She asked me to just forget about the situation, that she was moving on, and she was sorry she ever brought it up."

Frowning, Livy shook her head. "Why would she say that? Even if she's no longer pregnant, there needs to be some resolution."

"I think so, too," said Austin. "We'll tackle that problem later. Right now, we need to get your mother to the airport."

"I heard that," said Livy's mother walking onto the porch. "I do appreciate the ride to the airport. It gives me a chance to thank you for all you've done for Livy following that awful incident with Wayne."

Austin shook his head. "If that guy ever comes close to Livy again, I'll do more than punch him. I'll call the police. He's a low life who thinks he can get away with stuff like that. I've done a little research, and Livy isn't the only one he's abused."

"Maybe someone should report him to the school," said Livy's mother.

"I don't want to deal with that," Livy said quickly. Some might call her a coward, but there was more to the story. This was one of those "he said, she said" situations. What proof did she have that Wayne physically attacked her? She'd been in shock after it happened and hadn't called the police or told anyone. Fear and humiliation kept her silent. At this point, she just wanted to put it behind her.

Austin checked his watch. "I think we'd better leave. Traffic is terrible."

They loaded Livy's mother's suitcase and climbed into Austin's convertible.

"I've kept the top up so you ladies wouldn't ruin your hairdos," Austin said.

"Thank you," said Livy's mother, while Livy just laughed. The wind would do no worse on her curls than the heat and humidity.

On the drive, Livy's mother spoke to Austin about the loss of his mother. "I met her just the one time, but she was memorable. I'm sorry her life ended too soon."

Livy wondered what he would say. He'd been working through his anger that she'd overdosed without giving him the chance to reconcile with her.

"I'm sorry too. She wasn't an easy person to get along with, but she was my mother," he said.

"Families can be complicated," Livy's mother said.

Livy knew she was referring to Livy's birth father, who basically had written both her mother and her off. But her stepfather, Jack, was a kind, loving man who more than made-up for him.

By the time they reached the airport, Livy was confident that her mother and Austin had made a healthy connection.

Her farewell to her mother was full of gratefulness. They might not agree on some things, but they loved one another, and Livy was confident Austin would be truly welcomed by her family.

As they pulled away from the airport terminal, Livy turned to Austin. "Okay, now tell me about this phone call from Aynsley."

"Aynsley is up to no good. I'm not sure what's going on, but I'm determined to find out. I talked to Shane and asked him to do a little research for me. I want to know how her ex, Laurence, fits into things. I have a feeling he's playing a part. Otherwise, why would he go to the hospital to be with Aynsley? And why would he tell me he wanted to help support the baby?"

"It's such a mess," Livy said. "Hopefully we get an end to it soon. How about your other phone call?"

"The one with a potential partner? I talked to an old friend, a fellow computer geek who's interested in developing a new formatting system for authors. It seems promising. A little bit like a program for Mac users, but this would be workable on all platforms. I'm trying to talk him into moving here. We'll see."

CHAPTER TWENTY-FIVE

ELLIE

Ellie strolled through a vineyard outside of Epernay in the Champagne district of France, deep in thought. She'd been ready to fly home for a while, then a note from Liz changed her mind. There was something going on between Austin and Livy—some kind of trouble. Liz didn't say what it was, but as far as Ellie was concerned, that changed everything.

She didn't want to return to Florida before all three of her granddaughters had solid plans for the future. She wanted to see Livy engaged to Austin. Then she'd be ready to return.

"Are you okay, Ellie?" John asked, walking up to her and placing an arm around her. "You've been standing here staring into space for a while."

Ellie shrugged off her worries and turned to him with a smile. "I'm fine. Just thinking of home. That's all."

"Are you ready to go back to Florida?" John asked.

Ellie shook her head. "Not yet. I can't wait to taste this vineyard's champagne. How about you?"

"Champagne, maybe a little nap ... or something before dinner," he said, giving her an exaggerated wink.

Ellie laughed. She'd play along with his plan. It led to others. Blushing at the thought, she took hold of his hand and they headed to the tasting room.

CHAPTER TWENTY-SIX

LIVY

Livy drove to Austin's house. Instead of going out, they'd planned a quiet dinner there. Since dropping her mother off at the airport together, it was the first time she'd seen him in a couple of days. Austin had been in Miami and was secretive when she'd asked what he was doing.

Full of curiosity, she parked in front of his house and bounded up the stairs, hoping to surprise him.

She stepped inside, and reeled back with surprise when Aynsley got up from the couch and faced her.

"Austin?" Livy called, feeling unsteady on her feet.

He came out of his office. "Hi, Livy. Aynsley is here to talk to you." He walked over to Livy and put an arm around her.

"I owe you an apology," Aynsley said, her voice shaking. "I did something that was wrong and believe me, I've paid the price for it. I've been trying to get Laurence back. One of the reasons we broke up was he wanted children and I didn't. I thought if he knew I was having a baby that would help convince him that we could work things out."

"But you told him the baby was Austin's. How was that supposed to work?" Livy said between clenched teeth.

"I knew if I told him the baby was his, he wouldn't believe me."

"You lied to all of us and hurt Austin's reputation to get what you want? You selfish ..." Livy choked on the words.

"But it worked. After Laurence came to the hospital to see me, the real story came out and now he wants to try for another baby with me." Tears rolled down Aynsley's cheeks.

She clutched her hands in a prayerful pose. "I know it was an awful stupid way to go about things, but after divorcing Laurence, I knew I'd made a big mistake and wanted him back, and I couldn't figure out how to do it."

"I heard he recently inherited a lot of money," said Livy sarcastically.

"It's not what you think. I do love him," said Aynsley sniffling.

"But what about Austin? That was an awful thing to do to a friend," said Livy, furious.

"That's why I'm here. I wanted you to hear the truth from me. Austin made me promise I'd do this for him. It doesn't matter about the DNA test. It wasn't Austin." Aynsley looked down and shifted from side to side. When she looked up, her expression was full of misery. "Nothing happened between Austin and me. I knew it was wrong to say so, but I was desperate. Laurence has been the best thing ever to have happened to me. If you think Austin's life was difficult growing up, mine was worse, with parents who never wanted me. That was part of the reason I didn't want children of my own. But that's all changed."

Livy glanced at Austin. His lips were pressed together with anger. Then he spoke to her. "The part about her parents is true. I was around to know some of it. That's why we remained friends."

"But I don't understand her lying to you and to everyone, hurting your reputation," said Livy. "It was such an unforgiveable thing to do."

"Oh, I know that. So does Aynsley. That's why we called a group of our friends together so Aynsley could tell them the truth with me present. I don't want anyone to think I'd do what she accused me of." He tightened his grip around her shoulder.

They turned at the sound of a car entering the driveway.

"Looks like Laurence is here right on time," said Austin. "You can go now, Aynsley."

Aynsley got to her feet and went to Livy. "I'm sorry. I really am. I know I need professional help, and I'll get it. That's another promise I've made to Austin."

Austin and Livy walked her to the door.

Aynsley dashed outside and over to the black Mercedes Laurence was driving.

Together, Livy and Austin watched the car drive away.

"I'm sorry for everything that happened," said Austin. "It's a pretty weird scenario, but then, Aynsley had more to lose than money, even though that's important to her."

"I wish I felt sorry for her, but I don't," said Livy honestly. "After spending time with my mother and knowing how much she loves me, I can't imagine how awful it must be to know your parents never wanted you or cared about you."

"That pretty much sums up her life," said Austin. "I thought of filing a lawsuit for defamation of character, but this way is much more effective. If in the future, we see either Aynsley or Laurence, we can simply walk away. What happened between us and them will finally be put to rest when I get the results of the DNA test."

"But you don't really need that anymore, do you?"

"It's just something I need to see. I know Laurence is waiting for it too." Austin cupped her face in his broad hands and gazed down at her. "I know you've felt betrayed in the past, but I hope you understand I'd never do anything to hurt you. You're too important to me."

"I trust you, Austin," said Livy. "With all my heart."

His lips met hers, and she felt a sting of tears at the thought of how much he meant to her.

When they pulled apart, Austin said, "It's been a tense time for us. Let's relax on the porch. How about a glass of wine? And then I'll grill a steak."

"Perfect," Livy said, and together they walked into the kitchen.

He stopped and looked around. "I was thinking of upgrading the kitchen and doing some other things to the house. What do you think?"

"I love the location and the bones of this house. With the land surrounding it, you can do pretty much anything you want to it, including putting in a pool and patio."

He grinned. "I like that. Are you willing to talk to an architect with me?"

"Sure," she said, wondering if this was his way of letting her know he saw a future that included her. But he opened a bottle of wine and said nothing more about it as they headed out to the porch.

Later, after dinner, they took a walk on the beach. The moon was a glowing orb above them, allowing its light to help them see as they stood at the water's edge and gazed at the silvery light on the water.

"Seeing this beautiful sight, I could almost imagine walking across the water," said Livy, indicating the scene in front of them.

"And where would it lead you?" asked Austin, smiling at her.

"To a magical place where everyone was kind and loving," she responded dreamily.

He turned her to face him. "But you already have found that place." His voice grew husky with emotion. "In you."

Livy reached up and hugged him. He was such a decent man. She couldn't wait to show him how much she loved him.

CHAPTER TWENTY-SEVEN

ELLIE

Ellie opened her computer with eagerness. She and John were now in England in the Cotswolds countryside town of Cheltenham. As beautiful as it was, Ellie was hoping that Liz's next message would mean that she could go forward with her plan to head home.

She read:

"Hello, Ellie,

"I've been wondering when you're coming home. It seems as if things are settled here. Austin and Livy are happy and together. Brooke and Dylan are talking about a wedding in a year in Santa Fe, and Charlie and Shane are getting more and more done in their new house. Adam is dating a sweet woman who happens to be Skye's preschool teacher and is the mother of a little girl Skye's age. The four of them look adorable when they're together.

"Sarah, Karen, Pat, and I miss you at our wine gatherings in the evenings, and I know Sam misses having John here.

"Come home. We miss you.

Liz."

Ellie hurried onto the porch of the B and B where they were staying, her pulse racing with excitement.

John looked up at her from the rocking chair where he was sitting and reading a book.

"It's done. We can go home now," Ellie said.

"Not until I finish this book," he said, grinning. "I'm almost there."

Ellie laughed. She loved him so much.

CHAPTER TWENTY-EIGHT

LIVY

A few days later, as agreed, Livy sat with the architect and Austin in his kitchen going over details of what Austin wanted done to the house. She felt a little awkward but didn't want it to show. She knew Austin loved her, but he hadn't asked her to marry him. He probably wouldn't for a while.

The architect, a middle-aged woman name Belle, was excellent at pointing out ways to increase storage and add features that would be both handsome and useful. Every time it came to a decision, Austin deferred to Livy.

"Livy is the person who liked this house from the beginning and knew how beautiful it could become," said Austin giving her a smile.

"Such a sweet couple," murmured Belle, making notes.

Livy and Austin exchanged glances but neither spoke.

After a final walkthrough of the house to discuss plans, Belle left with a promise to get right on the drawings and to coordinate with Adam, who'd agreed to do the work on his own with some subcontractors he'd met.

"It's going to be beautiful," Livy said. "And what a great way for Adam to start a business. I love how this is working out."

"I love you," said Austin, drawing her into his arms. "Thanks for helping me with this project. I do a whole lot better with computer stuff."

"That's important too," said Livy, accepting a kiss from him.

"What should we do tonight?" Austin asked. "Want to go

out to dinner?"

Before Livy could answer, her cell rang.

She picked up the call. *Brooke.*

"Guess what!" Brooke said without waiting for Livy to speak. "Gran and John are back. They surprised us a few moments ago."

"We're on our way," said Livy, ending the call and facing Austin. "My grandparents are back. We have to go to the cove right away."

Life was about to take a turn.

When Livy walked into Gran's house and saw her standing in the kitchen, she couldn't help the tears that formed in her eyes. Gran had always been a person who soothed Livy's fears, who comforted her when she needed it.

She ran into Gran's open arms. "Hi, I'm so glad you're here." She turned to John. "And you, too. Does Billy Bob know you're back?"

John gave her an impish grin. "Thought I'd surprise him tomorrow morning. Heard you two have become friends."

"He's the best," said Livy with feeling. This wasn't the time to get into the story about his confrontation with Wayne, but it was one big reason Livy would always be grateful to him.

"What brought you back early?" Livy asked. She glanced at Charlotte and Brooke.

Gran chuckled, "If one more person asks that, I'll think you don't like the fact we're home. But the truth was, I missed the cove and the Inn." She took hold of John's hand. "Still, we've had the most divine time for the past couple of months."

He smiled and winked at her. "Yes, we did. We won't bore you with too many photographs, but we took quite a few. And the food and wine? Fantastic! I bought a few local cookbooks to have on hand at the Inn. We might try a few new things."

"We have so much to tell you," exclaimed Charlotte. "But I'm sure you want to get unpacked and settled. There's plenty of time for that."

"We're hosting a small wedding here over the weekend. I think you should be prepared," said Brooke.

"So, it's true. Sanderling Cove weddings are back," said Gran, clasping her hands and facing them with sparkling blue eyes. "I'll get rested and then dig in with the plans."

Livy glanced at her cousins and waited for one of them to speak.

Charlotte gave Gran a hug. "Everything is taken care of, Gran. But you can sit in on our progress meetings. And, of course, you'll be part of the staff overseeing it."

"Oh," said Gran, looking deflated.

"Good thing we'll have time to get reacclimated," said John gently, putting an arm around Gran.

"Oh, yes, of course," Gran replied, giving them a smile.

Livy wondered if John would be as eager to get back into his usual kitchen routine, or would he understand that they'd all need time to get used to having him back. Livy's cell rang. *Granny Liz.*

"I'm hosting a cove party for Gran and John," said Liz. "However, sweet girl, I need your help. Sam is going to grill some steaks and the other women will fill in with salads and all. But can you bake something special for dessert? Will you have time to do that?"

"Of course," said Livy, pleased to be asked. Spontaneous occasions like this were fun, and she knew how much this group loved her individual cupcakes in different flavors. She ended the call and faced the others. "I've been called to duty. Granny Liz is hosting a cove party, and I said I'd help. I'll see everyone later. I'm going to do some baking."

"I'll walk you over to the Inn," said Austin. He shook hands with John. "Welcome back." Then he turned and gave Gran a hug. "It's great to have you here."

"You and I can chat anytime," said Gran.

Austin glanced at Livy, then nodded.

Livy got out the ingredients she needed and began to work. She'd mixed up a couple of different batters when John walked into the kitchen.

"Hmmm. I see quite a few changes. You sure we needed another new ice maker?"

"Welcome back, John. We've changed things around a bit, reorganized a few things to handle larger crowds for weddings and all. Go ahead and look around. I know how hard it is to let go of old ways, but Billy Bob and I think we've made things a little easier."

"I see," said John, and Livy's heart went out to him. A cook's kitchen was his or her own. But until Gran and John decided what they wanted to do about the Inn and needed their help, she and her cousins would go on doing what they'd done well all summer long.

John opened some cupboards, looked through the freezer and the refrigerator without a word, and finally said, "Guess I'd better go get unpacked."

"See you later," said Livy cheerfully, but she had a feeling John wasn't pleased with the changes.

Following social time with guests at the Inn, Livy hurried over to Granny Liz's house, excited to see Gran and John again. After feeling their presence a lot at the beginning of summer, she'd become used to doing things on her own, her way. She had a feeling a lot of diplomacy was going to be needed in the days ahead.

Party noise met Livy's ears as she approached the house. She knew how happy everyone was to have Gran and John back home. The five families of the cove had always been close, and with her grandparents' return, things felt more normal.

Austin met her at the door. "There you are. I got the results of the DNA test and as we knew, it wasn't me."

Livy felt a huge smile cross her face as she let out a sigh of relief.

He kissed her and led her into the kitchen where a bar had been set up. A number of people were standing there talking, more were outside where John and Gran were holding court, giving out bits and pieces of information about their trip as people asked questions.

A warmth filled Livy. This place, these people meant so much to her.

Austin brought her a glass of pinot noir, her favorite, and said, "C'mon, let's go outside. I want to hear about the trip."

She followed him outside and was pleased to see a chair available at a table near Gran. She slid into it and listened as Gran talked about some of her favorite places. It did Livy's heart good to hear the happiness in Gran's voice, see the relaxed look to her face.

Sam carried the steaks inside, and soon Granny Liz called out to everyone to come inside and get food.

The dining room buzzed with happy conversation as people lined up and served themselves from the buffet that had been laid out. Grilled steak, corn on the cob, tomato salad, a mixed-greens salad, potato salad, and rolls were displayed.

Livy filled a plate with food and carried it outside hoping to grab the seat next to Gran. Brooke beat her to it but pointed out an extra chair and helped Livy pull it up to the table.

Gran turned to her with a smile. "How are the musketeers doing?"

Livy chuckled and gazed at Brooke next to her and Charlotte seated opposite her. "We're doing fine. Can't wait for you to see all the changes we've made."

"I think you're going to be impressed," said Brooke.

"We've been busy," Charlotte said, grinning at them.

"Well, then, it'll be exciting to see it," said Gran. She took a bite of Mimi Karen's potato salad. "M-m-m, everything tastes delicious. There's no place like home."

"Did you get homesick?" Livy asked her, surprised.

Gran reached over and clasped Livy's hand. "I wanted to see everyone and know that all was fine, but John and I had a fantastic trip. It was everything he wanted and more."

Livy noticed Gran hadn't answered her question. Was it true, like Granny Liz had mentioned to Charlotte, that Gran was just waiting for Livy to get settled before coming home? If so, Gran might have to wait longer. Austin hadn't proposed, and it didn't seem as if he would anytime soon.

The party lasted longer than she thought. Gran and John were the first to leave as they were still trying to catch up to East Coast time. Then Brooke and Dylan took off, followed by Charlotte and Shane.

"Do you want me to continue to help with the cleanup?" Livy asked, though she was anxious to leave. She wanted to check on the Inn's kitchen to make sure everything was as perfect as possible for John in the morning.

"No, no," Granny Liz said. "You go. We're almost done. Karen, Sarah, Pat, and I are going to take our time finishing up with a glass of wine. You run along."

Livy looked for Austin but couldn't find him. And when she checked, his car was gone.

Concerned, Livy headed to the kitchen at the Inn. Austin

had been unusually quiet at dinner, and it wasn't like him to leave without telling her.

Pushing aside her worry, Livy walked through the back door into the kitchen and stood a moment looking around with a careful eye. John had grumbled a bit about changes, but what Livy saw was an improved layout, better, much needed additional appliances, and a room that sparkled with cleanliness.

All was quiet in the Inn. She dimmed the lights and turned to go, satisfied that she and the crew had done their best during John's absence.

A figure loomed in the doorway and headed to her.

Livy clapped a hand to her chest. "Austin, you scared me! What's up? Why did you leave?"

"I had to take care of something, but I'm here now. How about some coffee? I've brought two cupcakes to go with it."

"Okay," Livy answered. "I could use a cup myself." She went to the sideboard in the breakfast room, fixed two coffees, and returned to the kitchen.

Austin was sitting at the table. The cupcakes were on a plate nearby.

He stood as she approached and held the chair for her.

Smiling, she sat down and looked up at him. "Thank you."

"You're welcome," he said. "Now, let's eat." He held the plate in front of her, offering her a cupcake. "Go ahead, that one is yours."

She lifted the cupcake to take a bite and gasped as it fell apart in front of her. A small package wrapped in silver lay atop the bottom half of the cupcake lying on the table.

"What's this?" Livy asked, her heart pounding. She unwrapped the package and stared speechlessly at the small velvet-covered box.

"Open it," said Austin, his face flushed with excitement.

She lifted the lid. A large emerald-cut diamond, surrounded by smaller round diamonds set in platinum, twinkled at her from the ring's setting.

Austin knelt in front of her. "Olivia Winters, will you marry me? I love you and want to share my life with you. You make my days brighter and happier than I've ever been."

Livy covered her mouth with her hands and stared at him. She'd made herself think this wouldn't happen for a while. Now that the moment had arrived, she could hardly believe it.

"Well?" said Austin, giving her a worried look.

She blinked, realizing he was waiting for an answer. Tears stung her eyes. "Yes, Austin, I'll marry you. I love you."

He stood and pulled her up into his arms. "Oh, Livy, you are perfect for me. I want to spend the rest of my life with you. I promise I'll always be a source of support and comfort for you."

His lips met hers, and when she felt moisture on her cheek, she didn't know whether the tears of joy had come from him or her. Austin, her beloved Austin, was hers.

When they finally pulled away, Austin picked up the ring. "Let's try this on. The stone belonged to my mother, but I had it placed in a different setting, one I designed for you." He slid it onto her finger.

Livy stared at the sparkling jewels and then faced him. "It's beautiful."

"Not as beautiful as you," he said. "I've waited for the right moment. Tonight, when I saw our families around us and those cupcakes of yours, I knew it was time."

"Very clever," Livy said with a teasing smile.

"You know how much I've always loved your cupcakes."

"I hope that isn't the only thing you love of mine."

"You know it's not," he said laughing as he pulled her into his arms again.

Livy settled her head against his broad chest as she liked to do when they danced. But they didn't need music as they swayed back and forth.

"It's too late to wake up Gran and John, but I'm going to call my parents," said Livy, stepping back.

"They already know," said Austin, grinning at her. "I called them to ask for their permission. Your mother is waiting to hear from you."

Pleased, Livy shook her head. "I can't keep up with you."

Livy punched in a call to her mother. "Hi, Mom."

"Livy, sweetie, Austin called us. Has it happened? Are you engaged?"

Chuckling, Livy held up her left hand. "Yes, it's real and the ring is beautiful. Austin was so clever. He hid the ring in one of my cupcakes."

Her mother laughed. "He always has liked your baking. Congratulations! I'm happy for you. For both of you. Thanks for the call. I know you're busy. We'll talk again tomorrow. I want all the details then."

"Deal," said Livy, pleased by her mother's excitement. Her cell rang. *Brooke.*

"Okay, if we join you now? Charlotte and I bought some champagne for the occasion."

"Wait! You knew Austin was going to propose?" Livy said.

"Oh, yes. We helped him plan it," said Brooke. "He was very nervous."

"He was?" Livy glanced at Austin. He grinned at her as he lifted a cupcake to his lips. She laughed. "See you soon."

Moments later, Brooke, Dylan, Shane, and Charlotte rushed into the kitchen.

Sharing this special moment with them seemed so right.

Shane did the honor of pouring champagne into tulip flutes and handed them out. Grinning, he raised his glass. "Here's to my little brother and his soon-to-be bride."

"Wait! How soon-to-be?" Livy asked and set them off into gales of laughter.

"You'll have to add a ring to your cupcake tattoo," said Brooke, indicating the design on Livy's ankle.

"When you add a paintbrush by your shell," Livy retorted, pretty certain Brooke would turn that down. Of the three of them getting tattoos, Brooke had suffered the most.

"Okay," said Charlotte, "Let's agree not to do that again. We have to think of our weddings." She turned to Shane with a smile. "We're not going to wait too long."

"We just have to figure it out," said Shane. "Stay tuned."

"I say we toast ourselves, all six of us," said Brooke. "It's been quite a summer so far."

"But what about the Inn?" said Livy. "That's the big question. We have to see what Gran and John want to do. That's why we're all here."

"I would hate to see it leave the family," said Charlotte. "But I already have two clients and don't want to give up my new business."

"And I'll be working for Dylan with his galleries," said Brooke.

Livy glanced at Austin.

"You're free to make any choice you want," he told her.

Livy held up her left hand and wiggled her fingers. "My choice is you."

He wrapped an arm around her. "We have a lot to think about. But we'll do it together."

"Our worries may come to nothing if Gran and John decide they want to keep running the Inn. We could all help from time to time, right?" said Charlotte.

"Yes, but it takes more than parttime help," said Livy. She, more than they, worked at the Inn on a regular basis and had fewer opportunities to leave because of her job in the kitchen.

"Let's not spoil this," said Dylan. "It's time to celebrate."

"Hear! Hear!" said Austin, raising his glass.

After all the champagne had been drunk, Charlotte yawned. "I don't know about the rest of you, but I have to get to bed if I'm going to get up with Gran in the morning. She wants to meet early to begin learning what we've done while she's been gone."

Livy checked her watch. "I've got to go too. I can't let John beat me to the kitchen on his first day back."

They quickly took care of the glasses, closed up the Inn, and left.

"Let's go home," said Austin stepping outside with her.

Home. Hearing the word, Livy turned to Austin realizing what a deep commitment they'd made to one another.

"Ready?" he asked, his voice grown husky with emotion.

She nodded, as sure as she'd ever been of anything.

At Austin's house, Austin and Livy quickly got ready for bed and slid under the sheets of the king-sized bed in his bedroom. In the glow of outdoor light seeping through the window blinds, Livy studied the ring on her finger. It was gorgeous. More than that, Austin had taken the time to design the setting himself. That meant more to her than the size of the diamond.

"Did I do all right?" Austin asked softly, pulling her to him.

"You certainly did, but the ring is only as beautiful as the pledge behind it," said Livy. "I love you, Austin. I always will."

"That's the most important thing to me. I'm not sure what the future will bring, but we'll face it together. Including dealing with the Inn."

Livy snuggled up against him and closed her eyes, secure

in her love for him.

Much later, an annoying noise rang in Livy's ear. She stirred and, seeing the pale glow of early morning sunlight cross the room in lemony stripes, she sat up quickly, checked the bedside clock, and turned off the alarm.

She jumped out of bed, sprinted to the bathroom, and was fully clothed and ready in record time.

Austin stirred in bed. "What are you doing?"

"It's late. I'm leaving for the Inn now. Hopefully, John won't be there yet. Love you." She kissed him quickly, escaping the arm that reached out for her, tempting her to linger.

CHAPTER TWENTY-NINE

LIVY

As Livy pulled her car into the parking lot at the Inn, she saw John crossing the lawn to it. Pleased she had made it on time, she got out of the car and raced over to him. "Good morning. Welcome back to the Inn."

He grinned. "Couldn't wait to get started. I'm ready to take over."

Livy's smile wavered. The kitchen had become hers. She wasn't ready to simply hand it back. She'd hoped they'd work together while she showed John what they'd changed to the facilities as well as to their routines.

John placed a hand on her shoulder. "No worries. I'm here to learn what you have done in my absence. That trip meant more to me than I can say. It was perfect. And it wouldn't have happened if you three women hadn't agreed to help out."

Feeling more comfortable, Livy said, "Come inside. We have some time before the other staff members get here."

She led him into the kitchen and as she'd done the night before gazed around the kitchen with a sense of pride. She showed him the new icemaker, the second dishwasher, and some of the cooking items she'd ordered.

He remained silent.

She opened cupboard doors, grateful for the time she'd had to clean inside, and pointed out where some items had been placed. "It's a little different, but basically all the same items are here. I placed baking items in one place so I could easily get to them."

"How are the guests reacting to your cookies and cupcakes

and all?"

Livy felt a smile cross her face. "Everyone loves them. Especially Austin." She held out her left hand. "Look what happened. It was too late to wake you and Gran, but I want to be the first to tell you that Austin proposed last night after the party."

"I'm very happy for both of you," said John, giving her a warm embrace. "You two have always been among my favorites."

Livy pushed at him playfully. "You say that to everyone."

"Guilty as accused," said John, grinning. "But I mean it for every one of you grandkids. You'd better run and tell Gran the news. She'll be thrilled."

"Thanks, I will," said Livy. "Billy Bob should be here soon. I'll be right back."

Livy hurried over to Gran's house full of excitement.

Gran was in her kitchen when she arrived.

"Gran, guess what! Austin and I are engaged," Livy said, holding out her left hand.

"Oh, my! How thrilling! Last night I could see how the two of you are together, and I liked it. He's a wonderful man." She clasped Livy's hand and studied the ring. "He's got excellent taste too." She hugged Livy hard. "You both are going to be very happy. I just know it."

"It's been a busy summer with all of us getting engaged," said Livy.

"Just the way I'd hoped," Gran said, smiling at her. "It looks like we have a busy wedding year coming up. I'm excited for all of you."

"Me, too. Charlotte and Shane and Brooke and Dylan are perfect for one another." Livy realized it was true. Of all the cove kids, the best choices seemed to have been made.

"Now, we'll have to see about the Inn. John is excited to be back, and so am I."

Livy was worried that they might want things to go back to the way they were before she and her cousins arrived.

Charlotte joined them in the kitchen. "Is everybody ready to start the day? I need a cup of coffee, but I'll get that at the Inn. I can't wait to show you all the things we've done to it."

"Lead on," said Gran. She looked adorable in a tan pair of shorts and a pink T-shirt that said "*Buon giorno*"—good morning in Italian.

"I see you've kept up your T-shirt pattern," said Charlotte.

Gran chuckled. "You bet. Nothing better to wear when working around the Inn."

"We do hope you're going to find that some of the changes mean less work for you now that we have new programs and employees in place."

Gran held up her hand. "One thing at a time, please."

Livy looped her arm through Gran's. "C'mon. The Inn awaits you."

They started out of the house.

"Hold on, I want to see the sign out front. I noticed it coming in yesterday."

As the three of them headed to the front of the driveway, Brooke joined them. "Where are we going?"

"Gran wants to check out the sign with the new logo," said Charlotte.

"New logo?" said Gran.

"Yes, we've added a whole new PR campaign with it," said Charlotte. "We think you'll like it."

"I'm sure I will," said Gran sounding uncertain.

At the edge of the road by the entrance to the Inn's driveway, they stared at the sign. "Well?" said Livy, anxious to hear Gran's response. She hoped they hadn't worked hard just to have their suggestions disregarded.

Gran clasped her hands together. “The sign is handsome. We should’ve replaced it a couple of years ago.”

“And the logo?” asked Brooke.

Gran gazed at Charlotte. “That too. It’s a simple design but says it all.” Gran sighed. “I know now how John and I had let things go. Let’s see what else you’ve done.”

“I’ve got to get to the kitchen,” Livy said, giving her grandmother a kiss on the cheek. “But I’m glad you like what you’ve seen so far.”

She hurried away and rushed into the kitchen to find John talking to Billy Bob.

Billy Bob turned to her with a smile. “John was asking me how well we’re working together. I told him we were good.”

“More than good,” said Livy. “Billy Bob is the gem you told me he was, John. I’d trust him to do anything we wanted.”

Billy Bob shuffled his feet. “This little lady knows how to cook.”

Livy held out her left hand to Billy Bob. “Austin and I are engaged.”

“I’m not surprised, but I’m pleased for you,” said Billy Bob, giving a quick embrace and, stepping back, his cheeks flushed.

“Have you told John about the weddings? The cooking classes?” Livy asked Billy Bob.

John looked startled. “Cooking classes? What else have you kept hidden from Ellie and me? Huh, Billy Bob?”

“Don’t blame him,” said Livy. “Billy Bob was a great help to us. He also trained new kitchen staff. We had to hire some part-timers to help with events.”

“Wow! I guess I’ve missed quite a lot. But it’s all intriguing. Now, how about this morning. Okay if I cook with Billy Bob, Livy? How many guests do we have?”

“We’ve sold 25 of the thirty-six rooms, but we’ll be fully booked over the weekend,” said Livy.

"That's great. This isn't normally a busy time of year." John looked up as Gran, Brooke, and Charlotte entered the kitchen.

"How are things here?" Gran asked John.

"Busier than usual," John replied. "Seems as if our granddaughters just might have a knack for running this Inn if the time comes when we're ready to turn it over to them or someone else."

Gran went to Billy Bob and hugged him. "It's wonderful to see you. Thank you for all your hard work while we were gone. It meant a great deal to us to know you and Livy were handling the kitchen."

"Welcome back." He indicated Livy with a nod. "She and I work pretty good together. Don't we, little lady?"

Livy beamed at him. "We're an excellent team."

"Well, seems like things are fine here. Let's see what has changed in the main rooms," said Gran. "Brooke mentioned Dylan's help there."

"Yes, we've moved some artwork around," said Brooke. "And we've bought some furniture, but every expense has been recorded for your review."

"Including PR budgets," said Charlotte.

Livy heard the hesitancy in Charlotte's voice and realized Charlotte was as nervous as she and Brooke. She followed them into the dining room.

Gran stopped and stared. "Oh, my! You've painted it!"

"What do you think?" asked Brooke.

"It's a surprise, but I think I'm going to like it. Makes everything look nice and clean. And the room looks bigger with the light color." Gran twirled around, inspecting the paintings on the wall and the cups on the sideboard with the new logo on them.

Livy opened the doors of the sideboard. "We bought some crystal glasses for the weddings we've put on."

"The cost was recouped by the wedding fees," Brooke quickly added.

"Yes, I've studied the website," Gran admitted. "So, I know about some of these things, but seeing everything in person makes a huge difference."

"After breakfast service, we'll sit in the office and discuss some of the changes we've made in detail. Right now, we can expect guests for breakfast shortly," said Charlotte. "First, let me show you the menus we've printed up for guests' use. It makes it easier for the kitchen to follow up."

"I'm going to go check on things," said Livy. "Hope you're pleased." She gave Gran a hug and entered the kitchen.

Billy Bob looked up at her and frowned.

"How are things going?" Livy asked, studying the way John had taken over the main counter. "John, we already had some muffins in the freezer. All we had to do was heat them up."

"You know me. I like everything super fresh," said John, waving away her concern.

"But only a few people ordered muffins. There are orders for biscuits, though. Let me show you the new ordering system," said Livy.

"What happened to the order pads and the spike we keep the paper orders on?" John asked.

"Austin helped us set up a program to keep track of everything," said Livy. "We now have a digital history of orders and a better idea for inventory. Plus, it makes it easier in the kitchen to be prepared."

John was silent.

"I think you'll like it once you get used to it," Livy said sweetly.

"I'll try. It's hard to teach an old dog new tricks, as the saying goes," he said, trying to smile.

"You'll be fine," Livy said. She never thought of John as old, but this made her realize he was in his seventies and had to be careful of his heart.

With fifty-some people all wanting breakfast, the hours flew by. Livy stayed by John's side, showing him the new routine. But he was happiest when someone simply called out the orders to him as it had always been done in the past.

Billy Bob collided with John at one point. Livy held her breath as they both stopped and stared at one another. John quickly moved out of the way, but Livy could see he was uncomfortable.

At the end of the breakfast cycle, John went to find Gran. "Time to see what else has changed here while I've been gone."

Livy followed him into the dining room and then led him into the office. "Charlie and Brooke are meeting with Gran. Let's see what they have to say." She knew he was upset and hoped Gran would make him feel better about the changes.

When they walked into the office, Ellie stood. "Glad you're here. We just started our discussion on the budget. Thanks to our granddaughters, business is booming."

John pulled up a chair next to her and took a seat with a sigh. "Takes a little getting used to."

Gran placed a hand on his knee. "Now, John, we have to give ourselves time to adjust. I'm finding it a little difficult too. But I've seen and heard enough that going forward, things will be easier to handle, even with more people here."

"Yes, they've apparently streamlined things in the kitchen," John said, avoiding looking at Livy.

Livy swallowed hard. She'd worked diligently to improve the procedures there.

Gran rose and wrapped her arms around Livy. "Some people have a difficult time with change. John will settle down. We both appreciate what you've done. He isn't quite ready to admit it yet."

"I'm here listening to you," muttered John. He turned to Livy. "I'm pleased to see how well the kitchen works. I really am. Thank you."

Feeling better, Livy gave him a weak smile. They hadn't even discussed the cooking classes she'd begun or how the kitchen and Inn operated while a wedding was going on.

Brooke had printed up a list of items they'd bought and their cost so Gran and John could see exactly how the money was spent.

Looking at it, Gran said, "You really got a lot for the money."

"We wanted to make up for the cost with new sales," said Charlotte, "but it hasn't happened yet. I believe it will, though. Especially with extra events like weddings and dinners."

"Oh?" Gran said. "How many weddings have you put on?"

"Only six so far, but we have bookings for more," said Charlotte.

"They were beautiful, romantic," gushed Brooke.

"Except for the runaway groom," Livy said.

"Oh, my! You women certainly have been busy," said Gran. "I used to love to host small weddings, especially when we were starting out. Remember, John?"

He returned her smile. "Hard work, but a way to grow the business."

"We want to try to do some occasional dinners for locals," said Livy. "Maybe provide package plans for down times. We haven't done it yet."

"But you've held one cooking class," said Brooke. "And both locals and guests loved it."

"How many in the class?" John asked.

"Only four. And we made carrot cake. Really simple to start with."

He nodded thoughtfully. "I see."

"Well, we certainly have a lot to learn about the past few months, but I'm suggesting we take a break. Karen is making lunch for everyone, and I'm hungry," said Gran.

"You go ahead," said Livy. "I'm working on appetizers."

John's eyebrows shot up. "We usually just keep it simple, pretzels and peanuts."

"We've changed it up a bit and are using that time to promote business," said Livy.

"All three of us try to participate," said Charlotte. "We consider it PR work, chatting with the guests, making them comfortable, giving them a sample of delicious treats. We've gotten quite a bit of new business doing that."

"I see," said John.

Gran took hold of his arm. "Come along. Karen is waiting for us."

After they left the office, Livy plopped down in a chair. "I didn't realize it would be difficult for Gran and John to accept what we've done."

"They're going to love it when they get used to it," said Charlotte with more confidence than Livy felt.

Brooke faced her. "I know you're worried about John. For some men, their jobs are what define them. In this case, John is realizing that is changing for him. It can't be easy."

"But don't give up on all you've done or put together for the future, Livy. John will come around. And so will Gran," said Charlotte.

Livy gave her a quick smile, but she wondered how long it would take.

CHAPTER THIRTY

ELLIE

Ellie crossed the lawn to Karen's house thinking of the many times she'd done it. This time, it felt a little different. Maybe because her life at the cove felt out of control. She and John had desperately wanted to get away, but she hadn't realized how difficult it would be to face all the changes her granddaughters had made. They were wise changes, though, and by her reckoning just might have saved the Inn from slowly fading away.

Her job now was to convince John that he hadn't lost a life he'd once known; he'd gained it back in a new way.

Karen greeted them at the door with a hug. "Come in. We're all so happy you're home."

Smiling, Ellie returned her embrace. This, the love and support from the cove families, made it all worthwhile.

She glanced at John. He was smiling.

CHAPTER THIRTY-ONE

LIVY

For the next few days, Livy tried her best to defer to John in the kitchen. Even when she knew there was an easier way to do things. She realized how important it was for him to feel in control. After two days of arriving at the kitchen at her usual time and finding John there ahead of her, she decided to come in later than usual. It was a smart decision. John liked it, and it meant she could spend a few extra minutes in bed with Austin.

On this early September morning of Labor Day Weekend, Livy arrived at the kitchen ready to face a few days of an almost fully booked Inn. Charlotte had advertised a special holiday package, and to their delight, it had worked.

When she opened the door to the kitchen, she stopped, puzzled. The lights were off. She flipped them on and stepped inside. For a moment, she thought she was seeing things. Then a shriek left her lips. John was lying on the kitchen floor. She ran over to him. When he saw her, he sat up and grabbed his left arm.

"What happened?" she asked, noticing the sheen of sweat on his brow.

"I must've fainted. I feel terrible. I think it's a heart attack."

"Hold on. I'm calling 911." In a shaky voice, Livy did her best to relay information to the operator who answered.

Billy Bob arrived. "What's going on?"

"John think's it's a heart attack. EMTs are on the way." She wanted to cry, but knew she needed to be strong for John.

"What can I do?" Billy Bob asked.

"Go get Gran at the house. She'll want to be here. I'll stay with John."

Billy Bob left with surprising speed.

Livy clung to John's hand and whispered a prayer that he'd be all right. "Hang on. Gran's on her way." She heard a siren in the distance and drew a breath of relief.

John tried to get up when Gran rushed into the room, but Livy held him back. "Just rest. The EMTs are almost here."

Gran hurried over to them and knelt. "John, darling, I'm here. Help is on the way. What happened?"

"I was standing, and the next thing I know I was here on the floor. I think I bumped my head when I landed."

The EMTs arrived and hustled into the room with equipment.

Livy let go of John's hand and stood to get out of the way. Billy Bob helped Gran to her feet and stood aside with her.

As the EMTs took John's blood pressure and checked his vitals, the two men talked quietly to John. Then one of the men turned to Gran. "We're taking him to Northside Hospital in St. Petersburg."

"John's doctor is there," said Gran. "I want to go with you."

"I'm sorry. It's best if you meet us there," said one of the EMTS as he and the other man got John onto a gurney.

"I'll drive you," Livy said to Gran. "First, I'll grab both our purses. Billy Bob, we'll leave you in charge. I'll be back as soon as possible."

Billy Bob waved her off. "Don't worry about a thing here."

"Thanks." Livy dashed over to Gran's house and grabbed their purses before rushing out to her car. She started the engine and pulled up near the ambulance.

As it pulled away, Gran climbed into the car and faced Livy. "Let's try to keep up with them."

"I will," Livy assured her. It was early enough in the

morning that traffic would be light. "What did they say?"

"We're all guessing it was his heart and not a stroke," said Gran. "We'll find out more when we get there."

Though it didn't seem that way to Livy and Gran, they crossed the bridge at 150th Avenue, onto Alt. Route 19 and into St. Petersburg to the hospital in record time.

Livy dropped Gran off at the emergency entrance and parked the car.

When she went inside, she saw that Gran was talking to a receptionist. Gran finished checking John in and then joined Livy in the waiting area. "We won't be able to see him until they've run some tests." Her eyes filled. "If anything happens to him, I don't know what I'll do."

"It's going to be all right." Livy clasped Gran's hand and gave it a squeeze. "We're all here for you—now and in the future."

"I know, I know," Gran said sniffling. "It's just that John and I are finally married and are enjoying life. I thought we'd have more time together."

"Look at me," Livy said softly, but with authority. "John's going to be all right. He was alert and talking, and he's receiving excellent medical care."

"You're right," said Gran, "but I don't know what we're going to do about the Inn. I don't want him working there."

"One step at a time," Livy warned her. Inwardly, she hoped the changes in the kitchen hadn't added to John's stress, causing this episode. "I'm going to call Charlie and Brooke to let them know what's happened."

"Oh, yes," said Gran. "You go, and I'll stay right here."

Livy went outside and sat on a bench. Now that she was sitting, her body suddenly felt weak as her level of adrenaline subsided. When she'd first seen him, she'd thought John was dead. She clicked on Charlotte's number and waited for her to pick up. "Livy, my word! What happened? Brooke and I are standing here together about to call you."

Livy filled them in and then said, her voice, quaking, "Do you think it's because of all the changes I've made in the kitchen?" As silly as it might seem to others, she had to know.

"I don't think so, Livy. You don't want to go there. We all know that John was having heart issues. Let us know when you have more news, and please give Gran a hug for us. Call when you can. We're super busy here."

"Will do," said Livy. She ended the call and then phoned Austin. She knew he would make her feel better.

"Hey, Livy," he said when he picked up.

Livy told him about finding John on the floor.

"Do you want me to come there and be with you and Gran?"

"Not yet. We don't know what's happening or where he'll be." Tears stung her eyes. "I just had to hear your voice."

"I'm here, Livy. Call me anytime you're ready to have me come."

Livy ended the call and sat a moment. She realized how lucky she was to have found Austin. He was a man she could trust not to hurt her, a man who loved her.

When she went inside, Gran was still sitting in the waiting area.

"Any news?" Livy asked her.

Gran shook her head. "Not yet."

"Can I get you a cup of coffee? Something to eat?" Livy asked.

"I'm not really hungry, but a cup of coffee would be great."

Gran looked smaller somehow, and older. It made her wonder how much longer her grandparents could run the Inn and what that would mean for everyone at the cove.

###

After what seemed an eternity, a doctor approached them. With the waiting area empty, he spoke freely. "Are you here for patient John Rizzo?"

Gran and Liz jumped to the feet. "Yes, doctor. How is he?"

"Hello, I'm Doctor Watson. We've had a chance to get a better look at John. As you probably suspect, he's had a heart attack, a myocardial infarction. We've taken a look at the image of his heart and are recommending a procedure known as percutaneous coronary intervention (PCI). That will give us the opportunity to see inside the arteries to look for the location of the blockage that caused the heart attack."

"Is it dangerous?" Gran asked, her voice shaking.

"All procedures must be done carefully, but we have talented specialists on hand," said Dr. Watson.

"How long will it take?" Livy asked.

"One to three hours," Dr. Watson said. "But we'll keep him longer than that."

"May we see him?" Gran asked.

"Just one of you, for a few minutes," the doctor replied.

"Give him my love," said Livy, giving Gran a hug.

She watched Gran walk away with the doctor and took a seat to research information on her phone. After reading about it, she felt better. There was no doubt that John's life was about to change dramatically, but he was alive, and that's all that mattered to her.

She called Brooke to give her an update.

"How are thing going there?" Livy asked. "Breakfast should be about over."

"All I'll say is we miss you, Livy. Billy Bob has been great, but with the Inn almost full, it's been hectic. How are we going to continue with John gone?"

"That's something we're going to have to discuss," said Livy, feeling pressured to continue working at the Inn when she wanted to do something else.

When Gran returned from seeing John, Livy's concerns about her future evaporated. The spring in Gran's step, the way she usually carried herself, as if she were ready to take on the world, had disappeared.

"How is he?" Livy asked her.

"A little scared," said Gran. "He's going to be all right, but our lifestyle will have to change." She sank down onto a chair. "Until recently, we've always taken our good health for granted."

Livy took hold of her hand. "One thing I don't want you to worry about is the Inn. Charlie, Brooke, and I will continue until you decide what you want to do."

"Thank you, darling," said Gran. "That means a lot to me. We'll have to discuss all of that later. Right now, I need to make sure John gets well and stays well."

"In the meantime, I think we should get something to eat. You've only had some coffee. I could use some breakfast too."

They went to the cafeteria and sat quietly as they ate.

When they'd finished, Livy rose. "I'm going to call Charlie and Brooke and let them know what's happening. I'll go outside to do it. Will you be all right?"

"Of course. I'll go back to the waiting area. There, I feel closer to John." Gran shooed her away. "Go ahead. I'm fine," she said, sounding more like herself.

Pleased, Livy went outside, grateful for the fresh air.

Livy clicked onto Charlotte's number. She answered right away. "Hi, Livy. Any changes?"

"No, we're just waiting to hear how the procedure went. Gran and I just had breakfast. She's gone back to the waiting area."

"Why don't I come and replace you?" Charlotte said. "We need you back here. Breakfast wasn't as smooth as we'd planned, and we are having a big crowd for our social gathering. Billy Bob is still here, but he doesn't know how to make some of the favorites like you do. Besides, I really want to be at the hospital."

"I understand," said Livy. "It's only fair that you be given the chance to spend some time with Gran. I'll leave when you're here to replace me."

"Thank you. I really appreciate it," said Charlotte. "All I can think about is what is going to happen to them. Things will have to change."

"That's something we all need to think about. I hope I didn't speak out of turn, but I promised Gran that you, Brooke, and I would stay on until things were sorted out."

"Of course," said Charlotte. "We're family, and we'll take care of them and the Inn."

Livy felt a rush of love for her cousin. This summer had brought them close.

CHAPTER THIRTY-TWO

LIVY

Livy let out a sigh as she drove into the Inn's parking lot. It seemed as if many days, not hours, had passed since she'd discovered John on the floor. As soon as she walked into the kitchen, Billy Bob approached her.

"How is he?"

Livy filled him in on the details and then said, "But going forward, it'll be you and me in the kitchen. Gran is not going to allow John to go back to his usual routine. Are you willing to put in the same kind of time as you've been doing?"

"Sure thing," he said solemnly. "Guess we have a social tonight. Charlie told me it's going to be a bigger one than usual. Something about some of the locals being invited."

"I've got it under control," said Livy. "I've frozen some cheese puffs and made little meatballs already. I can handle the rest. But maybe it's time you learned some of these favorite recipes."

"Anytime," Billy Bob said. "Maybe tomorrow?"

Livy grinned. "Got some boating plans today?"

He laughed. "A few."

"Go ahead and leave. I'm going to be all right." She felt unexpected tears sting her eyes. "And John too."

"Yeah, I think so," said Billy Bob. "He's strong."

"He's not going to be happy with all the changes he'll undergo," Livy said.

"I'll get him on my boat, and we'll see how he likes that." Billy Bob gave her a salute. "See you later today. If anything changes, will you let me know?"

"Of course," said Livy. "You're family."

Billy Bob blinked rapidly and bobbed his head before turning on his heel and leaving.

Livy knew how touched he was and let him go. Then, she went to find Brooke.

"How is he?" Brooke asked, jumping to her feet from behind the desk where she'd been sitting.

Livy gave her all the latest details. "I already told Charlotte, but I want you to know I spoke to Gran about the three of us staying at the Inn until things get sorted out. I hope you don't mind."

"Not at all," said Brooke. "And, of course, we're going to help."

Livy hugged her realizing how many people had talked about all of them being family. It made her proud to be part of it.

As Livy headed to the Inn, Charlotte returned with Gran. A number of employees crowded around them.

Charlotte helped Gran out of the car, and she faced them. "John is through his procedure, and he did well. He'll be in the hospital for a couple more days, then after he comes home, he'll need to take it easy for several weeks. Thank you all. We really appreciate your concern."

Gran hugged those who came to her and exchanged further comments with others before Charlotte said, "Time to go home."

Brooke approached them. "You help Livy. I'll walk Gran home and then come help."

"Thank you, Brooke," said Gran. "You can help me call friends and family to let them know what's happened."

"Sure," said Brooke taking hold of Gran's arm before

heading across the road to Gran's house.

Livy turned to Charlotte. "How are things? Gran looks exhausted. Did you see John?"

"We were both able to spend some time with him. He's awake, and we were able to talk a bit. He knows things are going to have to change around here."

"I bet he wasn't happy about that," said Livy, recalling how displeased he was about changes in the kitchen.

"Gran isn't going to let him get away with anything when he comes home. She was shaken to the core to think she was about to lose him." Charlotte shook her head. "I can't imagine them apart."

"Well, we'll see that the transition works for them both. Now, we have to take care of the guests. It was a shrewd suggestion to invite local people to help sell them on the idea to use us for overflow guests and special events, but we're going to have to hustle to pull this off. All the food is prepared and ready to go. We have extra kitchen staff working, including Billy Bob who insisted he return for the event."

Charlotte placed a hand on Livy's shoulder and beamed at her. "I'm grateful you're in charge of this. Give me a few minutes. I'll go change."

Livy went into the kitchen. The gathering was due to start in twenty minutes, but they always had a few people come early. That would give her time to greet them while some of the food was heating.

Livy was chatting with a retired couple who lived down the road when Charlotte returned with Brooke and Gran. Surprised to see Gran, she excused herself from the couple and went to greet her.

"Gran, you should be home resting," said Livy. "We can handle this."

Gran's bright blue eyes flashed with a message of their

own. "Now look here. John had the heart attack. I didn't. I'll do what I want."

"Okay," said Livy, knowing it was best to let it go. "Just wanted to make sure you were up to it."

"I am. Thank you, darling." Gran waved to someone coming into the gathering room and went to greet them, leaving Livy firmly in her place. Admiring Gran's stamina and amused by her, Livy went into the kitchen to check on things there.

"The party was a huge success," Charlotte said, coming into the kitchen later. "How did we manage to go through all that food? You had to keep bringing out more and more."

"Good thing we had many items premade and ready in the freezer to defrost and use," said Livy. "But I agree, it was a success. The locals loved mixing with guests, and guests loved talking to locals about living in the area."

"More than that, we sold rooms," said Brooke coming to join them.

"For both guests and for local use," Charlotte added.

Livy had ended up being so busy in the kitchen she hadn't had a chance to be too involved with the crowd.

Several people were still gathered inside and around the pool deck and lanai, but cocktails and food were no longer being provided.

"This is when offering a dinner would be perfect," said Brooke.

"Hopefully that can happen in the future," Livy said. "How's Gran? She must be exhausted."

"She left a while ago, but she was having fun this evening. I was glad to see it," said Charlotte.

"I don't know about you, but I'm going to sit and have a

glass of iced tea," said Livy. The last of the dishes were being washed by staff, and she needed a break.

She was sitting with her cousins when Austin walked into the room.

Seeing him, all the emotions of the day struck her. She jumped up from her chair and ran over to him.

He pulled her into his arms and hugged her tight. "Pretty tough day, huh?"

"Yes. We were all scared about John and busy taking care of Gran and this party, which was a huge success."

"Why don't I take you home?" Austin said, gazing into her eyes.

"Yes, that's what I need." The fact that she now considered his house her home was meaningful. She had no idea what the future would bring; she just knew she'd be with Austin.

"Go ahead and leave," said Charlotte. "Brooke and I will see that everything is back in order. You've worked hard all afternoon."

"Thanks," said Livy. She gave them a wave and left the kitchen feeling as if her feet weighed twenty pounds each.

In Austin's car, she kicked off her shoes and leaned back. "Thanks for rescuing me," she said, smiling at him.

"Ah, I like being a knight in shining armor," he said.

"I wouldn't go that far, but I do appreciate it," she responded, teasing him.

Austin laughed. "But I haven't finished with the rescue."

"Oh? What do you have in mind?" she asked, playing along.

"Dinner to start with. But not until we've had a walk along the beach and a glass of wine. How does that sound?"

"Like you really are a knight in shining armor," she said, giving him a big smile.

"That's the way I like it." He reached over and squeezed her hand.

He pulled into the driveway and turned to her. "Come here, damsel in distress."

She leaned over, and he cupped her face in his broad hands and kissed her. The feel of his lips and the way he cradled her face, made her feel protected. Desire washed through her in waves and melted the stress of the day. She moaned with pleasure.

Austin pulled back and gazed at her with an arched eyebrow. "Maybe we can take the walk along the beach another time."

She laughed softly. It was exactly what she had in mind.

###

Later, lying next to him, Livy cuddled closer. Austin always made her feel loved, and treasured. She hoped that they, like Gran and John, would remain as close in the future as they did today.

"Austin? Can we talk?" she asked.

"Sure. Go ahead," he said into her ear, sending shivers through her.

She sat up. "I know our future is uncertain regarding jobs, which might affect where we live and what we do. But I have made a commitment to Gran that I'll stay at the Inn until things get straightened out. Is that a problem?"

He looked up at her and shook his head. "Not at all. A project I'm considering would mean we could stay right here. I intend to fix up this house regardless of where we might end up living. Does that make you feel better?"

"Yes. Even so, I'm not sure what I want to do. After a day like today, I'm not sure I want to remain at the Inn. But I won't let Gran down. So, until we know what she wants to do, I can't make any decisions."

He sat up and faced her. "Don't worry about it. Time will take care of any choices you might have to make."

"One day at a time. Right?"

He grinned. "One day and one night at a time. And each night we spend together is perfect."

She chuckled, happy to think of their future.

CHAPTER THIRTY-THREE

LIVY

The next few days were busy as guests came and went, but Billy Bob and Livy worked in harmony.

A quiet but heartfelt celebration took place when John returned home. Though he wanted to come to the Inn, Gran kept him quiet at the house even as people came and went to bid him well.

One morning, Livy walked into the kitchen and stopped in surprise.

"John? What are you doing here? I thought Gran said the kitchen was off limits to you."

"Sssh! She's still sleeping. Thought it was time to come see how things are going here. Should we order our quarterly supplies?"

"That's already been done. We do monthly orders now," said Livy.

"Oh. Well, how many orders do you have for breakfast? Do you need my help?"

Livy ignored his pleading look. "I'm not going to face Gran's wrath by encouraging you to stay. I'll fix you a cup of coffee or tea, if you wish, then I suggest you get back home before Gran discovers you here."

"I'm not a damn invalid," grumped John.

"No, of course not," Livy said in a soothing voice. "We just want you to get well and stay that way."

Billy Bob walked into the kitchen. "Hey, John. Here to help supervise?"

"Ah, no ... Ellie is going to kill me if she finds me here. But as soon as I get the go-ahead from the doctor, I'll be back. Wait and see." John gave them a little wave and left.

"What was that all about?" asked Billy Bob.

"John's dying to get back to work, but Ellie doesn't want him here. She wants him to wait until the doctor says it's okay."

"Fair enough," said Billy Bob. "But you won't hear me telling him to leave."

"I think we're all hoping the doctor will continue saying no," said Livy. "In the meantime, we've got to keep things going."

"Okay, little lady. Let's see what we have going on this morning. It's another busy one from the orders lined up."

"We're getting a little surge in bookings after the holiday weekend. Pretty soon, we'll be preparing for the family reunion. That's when we'll really be put to the test."

"It involves the whole cove group, right?" said Billy Bob.

"Yes, all the families and whoever we can get to attend. All of Gran's daughters and spouses and children will be here. Especially now, after John's illness."

Soon, she and Billy Bob were busy cooking breakfast for guests. Then, while Brooke worked with Beryl Pappas, head of housekeeping, and Charlotte worked in the office with the reservations system, Livy worked on breakfast rolls for the future.

Gran had yet to appear, which was something new for her. When she did come in, she told Livy to come to the office for a meeting.

As soon as she could, Livy entered the office to find Charlotte and Brooke already seated there with Gran.

"There you are, Livy," said Gran. "I didn't want to start the meeting without you."

"Sorry, I had to wait for a few things to come out of the

oven," Livy said, taking a seat facing her grandmother who sat behind the desk wearing shorts and a bright-green T-shirt that said "*Ciao*!"

"I've called this meeting to order to inform you that I am putting the Inn up for sale. John's heart attack was a big wakeup call for me. Also, seeing you three young, fabulous women giving time to the Inn when you are about to embark on exciting journeys of your own choosing made me realize how selfish it is of me to expect any of you to continue to help."

"Oh, no, Gran. We don't want to see it leave the family," said Charlotte.

"That would be awful for the cove people," Brooke said.

"We don't want the Inn to be sold to people who wouldn't take care of it like we would," said Livy. "Don't rush into anything. I told you we're here to help you."

Gran held up her hand to stop them. "I know you care, and so do I. More than you know. But the time has come to turn it over to others. I will keep you informed, but as of today, the Inn is officially on the market." Gran stopped talking and drew a deep breath. "That's all."

"But Gran ..." Brooke began. Again, Gran held up her hand to stop any talk. Back stiff, she left the room, but not before Livy saw the tears trailing down Gran's cheeks.

She turned to her cousins. "What are we going to do?"

"Right now, nothing. But after Gran is feeling better about this, I want to request that the three of us have some input on deciding about a potential buyer," said Charlotte.

"No wonder John feels left out," said Brooke. "I feel as if the breath has been kicked out of me. The Inn has become something precious to me."

"And to me," Livy added. "I didn't think it would come to this so quickly."

"I know my mother is against Gran and John running it.

She told me straight out. She also said that both your mothers agreed with her," said Charlotte.

"Probably the first thing they've agreed on in forever," said Brooke.

"With the three of them united, Gran had no chance," Charlotte said. "But for the first time since I don't know when, I agree with my mother. The Inn is too much for them to handle."

"It's been a lot for the three of us to handle, even with a knowledgeable, loyal staff," said Livy. She hadn't realized how tired she'd been until she fell asleep at the dinner table at Austin's house.

"Well, we've still got a wedding to do," said Brooke. "We can't disappoint the bride and groom."

"Maybe, my friend's cousin will have to cancel her wedding plans for next year, and I won't have to deal with her," said Livy gleefully.

"Who knows how long it'll take to find the right buyer?" said Charlotte. "Hopefully it'll happen before next year."

"Right," said Brooke. "Dylan and I want to be married and living in Santa Fe by next summer. But we've talked about moving there ahead of time."

"I'm not sure when Shane and I are going to get married. The sooner, the better, he keeps saying." Charlotte shook her head. "For me, anytime is fine to avoid a New York City society wedding."

"Austin and I haven't really talked about it," Livy admitted. "Our whole courtship has included one issue or another."

"Any word on Aynsley?" Brooke asked.

Livy couldn't help a shudder from rolling across her shoulders. "As a matter of fact, Austin heard she and her ex-husband, Laurence, are getting remarried. Can you beat that?"

"That's insanity. And now this business of selling the Inn," said Brooke. "No wonder you've put things on hold."

"Well, what do you say we take a few minutes and pamper ourselves on the beach," said Charlotte. "I could use some sun and relaxation."

"Great idea. I'll make a batch of fresh lemonade," said Livy. "I need some time to absorb Gran's announcement."

"Me, too," said Brooke. "I'll bring two umbrellas when I come out."

They left the office and hurried to Gran's house to change. When they entered the kitchen, Gran was sitting there alone.

"We're going to the beach for a while. Want to join us?" Charlotte asked.

"No, you girls go ahead. I'm going to watch a game of golf on TV with John," she said.

"Really?" Livy asked. "That doesn't sound like you."

"Anything to keep that man in line," Gran said. "I almost lost him. If I have to watch golf on television to keep him quiet, I'll do it."

Livy kissed her cheek. "I want to be just like you when Austin and I are married."

Gran laughed. "I have a feeling you are already. He's crazy about you."

"Like John is crazy about you," Livy said, pleased by the idea that she and Austin were already showing signs of a healthy, long-term marriage.

She went to her room to get changed. After grabbing suntan lotion and a beach towel, Livy went to the kitchen to fix the lemonade.

As she carried a thermos and three plastic glasses along with her towel and lotion, Livy thought back to the first time she and her cousins had sat on the beach together shortly after they'd arrived. Austin had come by with his brother. While

Charlotte had stared at Shane, Livy had tried not to gape at Austin. She'd had a crush on him since she was a teen. Seeing him for the first time in years, she'd felt a rush of attraction that sent a blush to her cheeks. He hadn't noticed. Or so she'd thought.

Brooke had set the two umbrellas close together, providing enough room for the three of them to huddle in shade. Livy spread her towel on the sand and sat. The sun was hot, but an onshore breeze made it pleasant. She stowed the thermos and a bag holding the glasses by an umbrella pole and got up. "I'm taking a walk."

Brooke looked up from the book she was reading and waved.

Charlotte was stretched out on a towel hiding her face under a straw sunhat and remained quiet.

Livy walked down to the water and as was her habit, stuck her feet into the lacey edge of the waves. The sound of them, the pull of the sand at her feet, and the cries of the birds worked together to ease the tension from her body. She exhaled a long breath and inhaled the salty air to let another breath out. Almost asleep on her feet for a moment, she jolted when she heard her name being called. She knew who it was before she turned to see Skye running to her. Livy held out her arms, waiting to hug the child who'd claimed her heart. She couldn't help wondering what a little girl she and Austin created would look like.

Skye ran right up to her, allowed herself to be hugged tightly, then stood back and looked up at Livy with a smile. "Guess what? I'm getting a brother."

"What? You are?" *Had Adam and his ex-wife produced another child when she was here?*

Adam walked up to her. "Hi. Nice to see you and your cousins relaxing for a while."

"Skye said she's getting a brother," Livy began, wondering about the story behind it.

Adam laughed. "Skye wants a brother, but I told her that the only brother she's getting for a while is a dachshund. We pick him up next week."

Livy chuckled. "That's adorable. I thought maybe you and Madison Mitchell had decided to get married like the rest of us at the cove."

"Not yet, but I've been thinking about it," said Adam, looking happier than she'd seen him all summer.

"The grandmothers will be so pleased," said Livy.

Adam chuckled. "Oh, yes. Whatever magic they have, it seems to be working."

"What a summer it's been," said Livy. "But I'm happy for you."

"Thanks. Me too. 'Glad John's okay."

"Yes, but in case you haven't heard, Gran and John are selling the Inn." Even as she said the words, Livy choked up.

"I'm sorry," said Adam softly. "I can't imagine what it's going to be like to have someone else running it."

CHAPTER THIRTY-FOUR

ELLIE

As she had for many years, Ellie hurried across the lawn to Liz's house for a late afternoon get-together with the other women of the cove.

"Instead of iced tea, I have a sparkling rose wine for us," said Liz as Ellie mounted the steps to her porch. "I figured we'd better have something to lift our spirits."

"Yes," said Sarah sitting beside Liz. "It's a sad day for all of us, but, Ellie, we understand completely your wish to sell the Inn."

"We're just hoping you find someone nice to buy it," said Pat.

Ellie sank down into one of the rocking chairs that formed a circle and sighed. "It wasn't an easy decision to sell, but I think it's the right thing to do. Otherwise, my granddaughters will be held back from making their own plans. They're just about to start married life, and I don't want to do anything that would interfere with that. Perhaps I never should have had them take over the Inn. Now they feel bound to stay until it's sold."

"But by having them come and help you, each woman has found love. That's something we were all hoping for," said Karen. "My Dylan is the happiest he's ever been, and it's because of Brooke."

"Both Shane and Austin have found the happiness I wished for them for years," said Liz. "You don't know what that means. If you hadn't invited Charlie and Livy here, along with Brooke, that might never have happened."

"Yes. Bravo to you," said Sarah. "It's been a terrific summer for all the grandkids."

"True," agreed Pat. "Even though my grandkids weren't here for most of it, their visit was wonderful."

"Okay, ladies. Time for a little wine," said Liz. She took the open bottle from a bucket of ice and poured them each a glass. After passing them out, she lifted hers. "Here's to the women of Sanderling Cove. We've stuck together through thick and thin. We'll make this sale work for all of us."

Ellie lifted her glass along with her best friends hoping Liz's words would come true. Because there was something else she needed to discuss.

After they'd all taken a couple of sips of the bubbly wine, Ellie cleared her throat. "I need to confess something. For years, John and I have thought of ourselves as being younger than we are. Now, it's really hit home that we have to slow down. We plan on staying here in the cove, but I must think of the future. Karen and Sarah, you've been alone now for a while. How am I going to be able to change my life?"

"You take it one day at a time. The fact that I live here at the cove with all of you supporting me made a world of difference after Joel died," said Sarah. "It still does."

"You still have John," said Karen softly. "My advice is to relax and enjoy each day with him and store those times for happy memories."

"I guess I'm rushing into things," said Ellie. "It's just that both John and I have lived our lives together at the Inn. It's going to be awful to see it go to someone else."

"Maybe you can work out a deal for you to manage the place after you sell it," said Pat.

"No, that would mean John would want to work there too," said Ellie. "An outright sale is the best idea. But thanks for your input."

"Time for some more wine," said Liz. "And then on to a happier subject. Ellie, are you going to be ready for your family party in a couple of weeks?"

Ellie felt her lips curve. "I can't believe it. All three of my daughters will be here at the same time. It's bound to be fun."

"And interesting," said Liz, making Ellie laugh. They all knew about family gatherings. They could be either good or bad.

CHAPTER THIRTY-FIVE

LIVY

Livy sat in the office with her cousins and listened as Jake explained the procedure going forward.

"Even through this time of uncertainty, we don't want to slow any of your promotions and other efforts to continue to show a strong business. The more successful the business; the higher the price we can establish for a sale."

"What about the wedding business? Brides reserve space months ahead of their wedding dates," said Brooke. "And we take deposits on the rooms."

"Good point," said Jake. "But you have a contingency clause in all of them in case something like this happened. In all honesty, we need to warn brides that there is uncertainty going forward—certainly those brides who have scheduled for next year. I think we can accommodate any weddings planned for this year. Sales can take time."

Jake cleared his throat. "As the person Ellie and John have put in charge of the sale, I will keep all information on prospects confidential and on a need-to-know basis. I've heard of too many deals going sour because bits and pieces of news got out. Not that your grandparents or I don't trust the three of you. It's just good business practice."

"I agree," said Charlotte. "It's going to be hard enough to focus on business without worrying about that."

"Ellie is speaking to the staff this afternoon to be clear about what any sale might mean to them. They definitely will be part of any negotiations Ellie has in selling the property."

"May I ask if you have any prospects in mind?" said Brooke.

Jake shook his head. "Not at the moment. But this is a nice property. And with the help you've given Ellie and John, it will show well. Your work this summer has made a big difference for your grandparents. You should be very proud of yourselves."

Livy glanced at Brooke and Charlotte, and grinned. They'd all done their best to make improvements to the property and guest services.

"Thanks for meeting with us, Jake. I know how busy you are with your business," said Brooke. She grinned. "I also heard through the grapevine that you and your girlfriend are engaged."

Jake's cheeks flushed in a charming boyish way. "Happened a couple of weeks ago."

"There's something in the air at Sanderling Cove this summer," said Charlotte. "Congratulations."

"Yes, I'm happy for you," said Livy. She'd always liked Jake, appreciated how far he'd come from a troubled childhood.

"Thanks." He gathered his papers and stood. "We'd talked about having our wedding here. Now, we'll have to wait and see what happens, just like the rest of you. Excuse me. I have to meet with Ellie and John."

After he left, Livy faced her cousins. "We only have two weddings booked for the fall. Betty Sue's wedding was the only one for next year. Maybe that's a good thing."

"Definitely," said Brooke. "We'll have to return her deposit if she decides not to wait out news of a sale. But you know how it hurts to give money back."

"We have to keep moving forward like Jake told us," Charlotte said. "The next wedding is in two weeks. That will give Gran a chance to see what we've done."

"Later this week, let's meet with her. She's been looking forward to it," said Livy. She turned to Brooke. "How are things with your mother? Is she still bringing her fiancé to the family party?"

Brooke smiled and nodded. "Mom sounds like a teenager in love. It's a little weird because that's how I'm feeling with Dylan."

"I love when stories like this happen," said Charlotte. "It's going to be fun to have the whole family together. Gran is ecstatic that everyone is coming."

"I want everything to be perfect," said Brooke.

"I'm trying to come up with some creative menus," said Livy. "And Mimi will help me. The other families will also be included in the festivities."

"And Adam and Skye," said Brooke. "They live here now."

"Oh, yes. You know Gran. She won't leave anyone out," said Livy.

"Who's signed up to stay at the Inn?" Charlotte said. "I know my mother and stepfather are staying here."

"My mother and her fiancé are too," said Brooke.

"My parents and two brothers are staying at the Inn," Livy said. "That makes just four guest rooms. That should make it easy."

"Or not," said Charlotte, and they all laughed.

That afternoon, Livy stood with her cousins along the wall of the dining room as Gran spoke to the thirty members of staff gathered there. Livy had made cookies and set out plates of them on one of the tables, along with a selection of cold drinks and water.

"And to reassure you, I've made staff retention part of any sales agreement. That isn't a guarantee, mind you, but what I hope will be a good outcome for all of us." Gran's shoulders slumped and when she spoke it was with a tremor in her voice.

"Some of you, like Beryl and Amby, have been with us since the very beginning. You're more than employees. I love you all."

Charlotte went to Gran and hugged her.

Livy went to the kitchen for more cookies. The ones she'd placed out had been devoured.

Brooke followed her and helped fix another tray of cold drinks. It was a nice occasion for the employees to be able to enjoy being together, even if the news wasn't great.

As Livy told Austin that night, "It felt almost as if a divorce was being announced and a family broken apart. But Gran will try to get a new owner to keep as many employees as she can.

"I remember some of the staff from when I was a teenager," Austin said. "It's going to be a whole lot different when strangers take over the Inn. No wonder Gran was emotional."

"Are you okay with putting things on hold for us?" Livy asked. "We haven't really talked about the future except to say we want to stay here."

"I'm as happy as I've ever been. If that means waiting to be married, I'm fine with it. More importantly, how are you with those plans?"

"I want to enjoy every moment of being engaged to you," said Livy. "My mother will still try to plan things, but as long as we're together, I don't care about anything but that."

Austin smiled as he bent his head to kiss her. "That's my woman."

She laughed, and eagerly met his lips.

The next day, Livy met with her cousins and Gran to discuss the upcoming wedding.

Gran listened as they explained the procedures they'd set up. "Using Rosalie at Tropi-Flowers is brilliant. She's easy to work with and very clever."

"You should see the floral ropes she makes," said Brooke. "They're stunning."

"She also gives us a special deal on flowers used in the Inn," Charlotte explained. "She's featured on our website, and we're featured on hers. A win-win situation for both of us."

"Yes, that makes sense," Gran quickly agreed. "I love your creativity. To be honest, John and I were too tired to want to work weddings. They can be so exhausting."

"The three of us working together makes it much easier," said Livy.

"You've done a fabulous job," said Gran. "Who knew there was true hotel spirit in each of you?" Her expression changed, grew more serious. "Jake and I toured the property. It's amazing how the changes you've made have created a far more attractive property. Thank you. It's going to mean a difference to us financially."

Charlotte, the ringleader of the trio spoke. "We each have benefitted from helping you this summer in meaningful ways. But we all wanted to help. I think I speak for all of us. You've been our rock throughout our lives."

"Amen," said Brooke.

"Yes," said Livy quietly, trying not to cry. Austin was the one she trusted to keep her feeling secure, but Gran had always been a solid foundation in her life.

On the day before the wedding, Livy, Charlotte, and Brooke went over the checklist with Gran. Fifteen guest rooms had been booked for wedding guests. Brooke had already given Beryl instructions for the housekeeping staff to place welcome baskets in each room before arrival.

Brooke showed them all the cute things that had been

placed in each basket. Some were gifts the bride's family had sent; others were items that Brooke had bought either online or locally. Each basket was festooned with gray and white ribbons—the color scheme the bride had chosen for her wedding.

"Who put these together?" Gran asked, looking at Brooke.

Brooke grinned. "I did. I love doing work like this."

"Such changes in you, but I love it, darling," Gran responded.

At the same time the baskets were placed in the rooms, plates of cookies and bottles of water would be added, along with promotional materials Charlotte had put together.

That evening, their time would be divided between guests of the Inn and the bridal party. With the weather ideal, the bride had requested an outdoor gathering. If a regular guest at the Inn sometimes mingled with the others, it usually was no problem. Still, Livy and the other women would try to keep that from happening.

The bride this time was a woman in her fifties who had reconnected with an old boyfriend, and they now were given a second chance. Though Livy suspected it would be a quieter affair than some, the guests who arrived for the weekend seemed excited about the event. The bride, Lisa Mackey, was a pretty woman who'd complained about the difficulty she'd had finding a dress she liked, but Livy knew it wouldn't matter what Lisa wore. Her fiancé, Jacob Huntsman, a tall, thin man who owned his own shoe company, gazed at her with such adoration it was touching. Rather than a fancy wedding outside Philadelphia where Lisa lived, they'd chosen to do something simple in a setting they both loved. Livy was thrilled that the gorgeous weather was holding because she wanted to make their day perfect for them.

That night as she circulated among the wedding guests

chatting with them, Livy recalled the time Austin had pushed Wayne into the pool. Remembering how terrified she'd been, Livy couldn't help looking over her shoulder to see if that horrible man was behind her. Her nightmares about Wayne had ended, but thoughts of seeing him again still unsettled her.

She saw Gran was chatting with a group of guests and didn't interrupt. She went over to the bride, who was standing and talking to her daughter, who was to be her maid of honor. Seeing them together, knowing of their love for one another, Livy was touched. They were more like sisters than mother and daughter.

"Lovely party," Lisa said. "The food is delicious. I'll have to tell a couple of friends of mine. People think because you have grown children you can't fall in love and get married. Jacob and I are proof that you can."

"It's really a wonderful story," said her daughter, Terri. "They've known each other since grade school."

Livy sighed. "Romance like that is very precious."

"I see you're engaged," said Lisa. "When are you getting married? And will you have your wedding here at the Inn?"

"I don't know," Livy replied honestly, though it hit her that with a new owner in charge the thought of being married at the Inn wasn't appealing. "We're still in the planning stage."

She moved on to other guests, but the nagging uncertainty followed her.

CHAPTER THIRTY-SIX

LIVY

When Livy stood outside early that morning, the sun was just beginning to rise from the horizon, sending rays of hope as well as lemony sunshine into the atmosphere. The wedding was important to her because she wanted to show Gran what they'd accomplished in a short period of time. Though work was required to pull off any wedding, the Inn's setting proved to be a perfect backdrop for this important day in a couple's lives.

She ran to the water's edge and breathed in the salty air hoping to settle her thoughts. After understanding what a change in ownership would do to her own wedding plans, Livy realized how conflicted she was about the Inn being sold. She didn't want to open a bakery, but she needed plans of her own for the future. She knew Austin could support them both, but she was used to being independent.

She looked down at the tiny fish darting about in the shallow water as if they had to worry only about finding something to eat. A wave washed over her ankles leaving salty kisses behind. This, standing here in the water enjoying a taste of nature, was something she knew she couldn't leave. She watched a trio of pelicans skim the surface of the water and was reminded of all she and her cousins had done together this summer—a trio of their own.

She thought of Austin and how much she loved him. Like a perfect shell, he was a gift she'd treasure. She'd had a crush on him years ago, but what she felt now was much stronger and deeper.

She heard a car approaching and ran back to the Inn to greet Billy Bob. She was glad they'd become friends who relied on one another to make the kitchen work. More than that, he'd once protected her. An act she'd always remember.

"How's it going?" Billy Bob asked her as they walked inside the kitchen together and turned on the lights.

"Last night went well. It's such a pleasant group of people that it's a joy to serve them," said Livy. "I want today to go smoothly. Right now, we have a wedding breakfast to put on in addition to our regular guests, a lot of whom came from Tampa and Orlando for a weekend at the beach."

"No problem, little lady," said Billy Bob, bringing a laugh from Livy. Only someone like Billy Bob could get away with addressing her like that. They both knew it, too.

The breakfast buffet set up in the private dining room looked especially nice with the orchid centerpiece Rosalie had put together. After breakfast, they'd place the centerpiece on the table inside the gazebo where the ceremony would take place. The arrangement of mini calla lilies, white roses, and white orchids was stunning. Livy knew from the planning sheet for the wedding that Lisa had ordered the same flowers for her wedding bouquet and a smaller one for her daughter who'd stand up with her. Jacob's cousin was acting as best man.

Charlotte joined her. "Everything looks beautiful."

"I take care of the food," said Livy, "but it's always fun to see the room before people arrive."

"We're off to a good start," said Brooke, looking over at them from one of the tables. She finished folding and placing the last white napkin at the table covered in a gray linen tablecloth to match the wedding color scheme.

As soon as the breakfast was over, they'd set up for the dinner that evening. Livy wouldn't be involved with that task. She'd be too busy cooking in the kitchen. Gran had agreed John could sit and watch while she did her job. His presence put added pressure on her, but she liked the opportunity to show off her skill to her grandfather, who'd encouraged her to cook from the time she was a child.

The breakfast went well, both in the dining room and in the breakfast room where regular guests had their meal. Gran and Charlotte handled greeting them and making sure all was in order while Brooke talked to the wedding crowd in the dining room.

After breakfast, Lisa and her female guests left to do some shopping while the men went on a short fishing jaunt. Beryl and the housekeeping crew took advantage of the unoccupied rooms to clean them and place another hostess gift inside.

Livy was in the kitchen preparing poached salmon when John came in. She and the kitchen staff gathered around him. "Welcome. We're glad to see you here. Sit down."

Billy Bob waved John over to him and held a chair out.

Grumbling softly, John went to it and sat. "No need to treat me like an old man."

"No way," said Billy Bob. "We're giving you the seat of honor."

Livy smiled at the two of them. They were buddies from way back when John first hired Billy Bob out of prison. Nothing would change that friendship. Billy Bob was devoted to both John and Gran.

She went back to work wondering how long it would be before John was on his feet giving her directions.

Too soon, she worked to keep her sense of humor as John thought she needed to add more seasoning to the steamship roast she was preparing, and then said the potatoes weren't sliced thin enough for the casserole. When she was icing the cake and John thought it could use a few more flowers, Livy was forced to hold her tongue. She knew exactly how many flowers she wanted on the cake. But then she also knew how hard it was for him to be unable to participate.

Gran walked into the kitchen. "Okay, John, let's give Livy a break. Will you walk me over to the house? I'm going to rest before the festivities start."

While John got to his feet, Gran turned and gave her a wink.

Livy returned her smile, grateful for Gran's understanding.

As they always liked to do, Livy and her cousins dressed up to help with weddings, thinking it added to the elegance of the occasion.

Standing in her bedroom at Gran's, Livy studied herself in the mirror. Over the course of the summer her skin had browned, and her strawberry-blond hair had lightened. But it was the happy glow on her face that Livy focused on. Thinking of Austin, the glow seemed even brighter.

She pulled on the black-linen sleeveless dress that had become a staple. She added the silver necklace Brooke had given her from her trip to Santa Fe. They and silver dangling earrings completed her outfit.

She met Brooke and Charlotte in the kitchen, and they went over to the Inn together. Amby and his nephew, Rocco, who worked with him, had set up chairs on the lawn outside the gazebo with a wide path between them for the bride and her father.

A harpist was setting up inside the gazebo. The minister was standing at the table looking at written notes.

When she and Charlotte went inside the Inn, wedding

guests were assembling in the gathering room waiting to go outside together.

Livy hurried to the kitchen to make sure Billy Bob had the appetizers ready to go. Cocktails and hors d'oeuvres would be served outside on the pool deck.

After seeing that the kitchen was in order, Livy went to the dining room to check on the buffet table. It was ready to receive food when the time came.

She helped guests find chairs outside and then stood with Gran, Charlotte, and Brooke as the seated guests waited for the maid of honor and the bride to appear.

Inside the gazebo, Jacob and his cousin stood to one side of the minister.

Terri walked down the aisle with her boyfriend. Dressed in a gray silk sheath and carrying a bouquet of white flowers, she looked beautiful. Her dark hair, like her mother's, and green eyes were offset beautifully by the gray color. The music ended as Terri stood in the gazebo on the other side of the minister.

The harpist began to play the popular wedding processional song by Wagner. Hearing the *Here Comes the Bride* melody on the harp sent a shiver of excitement down Livy's back. She imagined what her own wedding might be like. Lisa appeared wearing a white, tea-length sheath dress with a sheer lace crew-neckline overlay with long sleeves. It was, Livy decided, perfect for Lisa. Elegant, simple, and suitable for a small wedding. She glanced at Jacob and was touched to see that he was visibly moved by the sight of his bride.

Lisa's father climbed the steps of the gazebo, delivered her to Jacob, and rejoined his wife in the first row of chairs.

The table inside the gazebo had been moved close to the front so people in the audience could see and hear clearly.

Livy listened as the minister spoke the customary phrases

of the ceremony. Then she leaned forward to hear the vows exchanged between Lisa and Jacob. Their talk of long-lasting love, caring for one another, and other traditional statements touched an emotional chord. She and Austin didn't need a fancy ceremony; they'd already exchanged such words.

The ceremony was short but special, everyone agreed, as they rose from their chairs on the lawn to walk into the Inn for cocktails by the screened-in pool. Livy brushed past them to help put out the appetizers on a table in one corner of the space while a bar set up was at the other end to keep the crowd circulating.

Brooke was handling the regular guests while Charlotte and Gran helped the wedding guests. This tandem way of serving worked well.

When it was time for the wedding guests to come inside for dinner, they walked into the dining room where food was displayed on a buffet table. A small bar sat at the far end of the room. The four tables of eight were placed between the buffet and the bar and looked gorgeous with light-gray linen table cloths, shiny silver, sparkling crystal glasses, and centerpieces of white lilies and orchids.

The buzz of pleasant conversation filled the room as people lined up to be served at the buffet table. Livy watched carefully to make sure there was plenty of food. The wait staff, headed by Holly Willis, who'd gone from a part-time waitress to being in charge of wedding staff, was quietly and professionally doing their job.

Livy was pleased to see how well the whole evening was going. Gran seemed impressed.

When the three-tier wedding cake was rolled into the dining room on a serving cart, everyone applauded. At Lisa's request, Livy gave a quick wave and urged everyone to enjoy themselves.

While they were eating, Livy escaped to the kitchen to check on the status of things there. With two dishwashers, many items could be placed inside, but certain things like the pots and pans had to be done by hand.

"Do you need any help?" Gran asked, coming in to see her.

"Let's check the gazebo to make sure we didn't forget anything there. Brooke and Charlie are searching the pool area and the gathering room for glasses."

Gran gave her a little nod and left.

Livy was carefully putting away some crystal glasses when Brooke came running into the kitchen. "Gran's hurt."

"Hurt? What happened?" Livy asked, feeling dizzy at the thought.

"It's her ankle. She's twisted it. Badly. We need to get her to the hospital. Charlie is out front with her now. We managed to get her into my car. We need you to stay with John. I'll go to the house with you to get Gran's purse. She doesn't think it's a smart idea for John to come to the hospital. She thinks it'll be a strain on his heart."

"Oh, no. He'll be upset," said Livy.

"That's why we need you to stay with him," said Brooke. "C'mon. Hurry."

Livy turned to the kitchen crew. "You know what you need to do." She turned as Holly entered the kitchen. "Holly, you're in charge. I'll be back as soon as I can. Gran's hurt, and I need to stay with John."

"Oh, I'm sorry. Of course, go to him. Don't worry about this. I've got it."

Tears stung Livy's eyes. Such simple words, but they meant a lot.

She flew out of the kitchen and went to Brooke's car parked outside. "Gran! Gran!"

Gran was sitting in the back with one leg extended on the

seat beside her. Her ankle was swollen, and with her shoe off, her foot was swollen too.

Liz studied Gran's white face and the pain in her eyes and felt like crying. "I'm sorry this happened, Gran."

"Just stay with John. He'll worry, but really, I'll be fine. It's these damn heels. I never should've worn them."

"Hurry, Livy. Go now so we can leave," said Charlotte.

As she ran to Gran's house, Brooke passed her going the other way, holding onto Gran's purse.

Livy slowed her steps. She knew she had to pull herself together or John would be even more annoyed about being left behind.

By the time she entered the house, Livy was calm and determined to keep a light tone to the conversation she wished she didn't have to make.

"Hi, John. Gran has hurt her ankle, and Charlie and Brooke are taking her to have it checked out. Gran said there was no need for you to accompany her. She's going to be fine."

"What? She left without me? Now why did she go and do something like that?" John gave her a steady look.

"Gran didn't want you to worry. I'm sure if she thought it was serious, she'd want you there. It looked like a bad sprain to me. Otherwise, she's fine."

"I told her not to get involved with the wedding. I told her to leave it to you three girls."

"It was important to her to see how things were being handled," said Livy coming to Gran's defense. "At any rate, she'll have the ankle looked at and be home as soon as she can. In the meantime, can I get you anything?"

"How about a beer?" John said.

"Are you supposed to ..." was as far as Livy got. She was stopped by the glare John gave her.

"Okay," she said. At least it wasn't a hot dog, or a steak, or greasy, fried food.

She went into the kitchen and grabbed a beer for each of them. The day that had started beautifully was not ending well.

Later, while John was napping, Livy returned to the Inn to make sure everything was in order there. Holly, bless her heart, had left the kitchen in excellent condition. When she went into the dining room, she discovered the room had been left in the same condition with fresh white tablecloths replacing the gray ones used for dinner. A breakfast buffet would take place there tomorrow morning before the guests were scheduled to leave.

Livy plunked down in a chair so mentally and emotionally exhausted she wondered if she could ever get up again. She loved the Inn, loved working for her grandparents, but knew it was a life she didn't want permanently. Still, she'd work here for as long as she was needed.

She heard noises coming from the gathering room, and when she checked on it, several people walked up to her. "How's Ellie?"

"She's at the hospital now. I'm sure she'll be fine. Thank you for asking." Livy hoped her words were true.

Before she could be stopped by anyone else, she left the Inn and hurried back to John.

CHAPTER THIRTY-SEVEN

CHARLOTTE

Charlotte and Brooke sat in the entrance area of the emergency room waiting for the physician attending Gran to speak to them. X-rays were being taken on Gran's lower leg and ankle. The physician, an older man, had been hesitant to say much until he'd seen the results.

When he finally appeared, he spoke quietly, confidently. "It appears that instead of a sprain, your grandmother has suffered a fracture. While it is not severe, it is enough to require her to wear a cast or special boot for 4 to 8 weeks. Because she is older, we'll recommend at least 8 weeks. But we'll monitor it over time, and that may change. An adjustable boot will accommodate the swelling in the area, which will last for several days."

"Will she be able to walk with the boot?" Charlotte asked, unable to imagine both John and Gran being able to slow down.

"It's best to keep off the ankle for the next several days, but wearing the boot will mean she can walk. She might want to use a cane for balance."

"Does she have to wear the boot at night?" asked Brooke.

"She can take it off at night, when resting at home, and to bathe," the doctor said and then shook his head. "I have a feeling that Ellie is going to pretty much dictate what she can and cannot do. I leave it up to the two of you to give her some guidance."

Charlotte and Brooke glanced at each other with a smile. He knew Gran, all right. Charlotte was relieved that surgery wasn't necessary. Still, she knew keeping track of both Gran and John's activities would require the help of everyone. With the family weekend a couple of weeks away, she hoped the worst was over.

CHAPTER THIRTY-EIGHT

LIVY

Livy was with John when Charlotte and Brooke brought Gran home. The loving look of concern between them was touching to witness. After all their years together, they were obviously still in love.

"Okay, Gran, we've got your pain medication here in the kitchen ready to take tomorrow morning," said Brooke. "I've put the pills right next to a glass, so all you have to do is get a drink of water. I've also underlined the important information in your discharge paperwork. It's all clear." Livy knew that Brooke had helped care for her mother for years. It showed now in how she was handling the details for Gran.

"Is there anything else we can do for you?" Charlotte asked. "Do you need help to get into bed?"

"No, thank you," Gran said, leaning against John. "You've all done so much to help, but John and I will need to come up with our own routines. I'm ready to go to bed."

John and Gran headed out of the room.

"Refreshments on the lanai?" Livy said. "I'll get some ready."

"Perfect," said Charlotte.

"I'm going to change my clothes. I'll meet you two there," said Brooke.

Livy put cheese and crackers along with some cold grapes on a dish, grabbed a bottle of wine and three glasses, and headed for the lanai. They liked to get together after a wedding to discuss details. This time there was more than a wedding to discuss.

"Are you going to be able to help out with the Inn this fall?" Livy asked Charlotte. "Gran won't be able to do much."

"Your house is redecorated and waiting for you. Are you willing to travel back and forth?" Brooke asked her.

"As long as I have my room here at Gran's house, I can do that," Charlotte said. "But honestly, I won't be able to spend as much time here as you might like. I have two new clients for my business, and I'll have to work around them. But I'll certainly try to block out time for special events. I've already marked the family party weekend on my calendar."

"I can remain here most of the time," said Brooke. "But I'll be doing some traveling with Dylan to art galleries. And after the New Year, I'll be planning for my wedding in Santa Fe and living there part-time."

"What about you, Livy? Have you and Austin made plans on where you'll live? The renovation plans for his house look fabulous."

Livy smiled. "I'm really excited about them. It's going to be beautiful. We've agreed to stay in the area. Right now, everything is up in the air. It's driving me crazy."

"I can't stand the idea of the Inn going to a stranger," said Charlotte.

"It all depends on who it is," said Brooke. "But I'll be unhappy if we've done all this work and the Inn is sold to someone who wants to change it completely."

"Me, too," Livy said. "Maybe that's what's bothering me most about having to sell the place."

"When the family is here for the party, it's our time to shine. Even though we don't know what will happen in the future, we've proved our success," said Charlotte.

"Running an inn sounds a little better than a bakery," said Livy, laughing. "My mother wanted me to get married right out of culinary school. Thank God I didn't."

"I think my mother thought I was going to live at home forever," Brooke said. "Life sure is full of a lot of surprises."

"I say we toast the three of us," said Charlotte raising her glass. "This summer could've turned out very differently. We've all been blessed."

The three women raised their glasses.

"To the musketeers!" Livy said before taking a sip. She, more than most, understood how far she'd come from the troubled woman she'd been when she first arrived.

The days following the wedding were relatively quiet. Gran and John didn't appear at the Inn, though Livy and her cousins reported to them on a regular basis.

For Livy, it was a time to complete the inventory of operating supplies and equipment Jake had requested. The work was made a little easier because she'd cleaned out cupboards and storage areas, but there was still a lot to account for with items hidden in nooks and crannies throughout the dining spaces, and storage rooms. She thought of it as a treasure hunt because like any household that hadn't been disturbed in some time, forgotten and unexpected items were discovered.

Brooke was working with Beryl on an inventory of housekeeping goods and supplies.

Charlotte was going through history on the Inn's computer programs and was working with Austin on finding proper storage for records that needed to be saved.

As the time for the family party drew near, the pressure to find a new buyer grew. Gran had told Livy that all three of her daughters were adamant that the Inn be sold as quickly as possible so she wouldn't have the worry of it. Livy was torn about the sale of the Inn but remained quiet. Gran and John deserved the time to relax in their waning years. But working at the Inn is what had kept them young and active.

CHAPTER THIRTY-NINE

ELLIE

Ellie sat with her friends on Liz's porch happy to be out of the house and with people with whom she could speak frankly. The four women who were her longtime and closest friends had shared happy times and sad. They'd gone through sickness and death together, celebrated triumphs both large and small, and knew they could count on one another for support. Today, she needed theirs.

"How are you doing being semi-retired?" Karen asked her.

"Not very well," she answered, her voice trembling in an uncharacteristic way. "The Inn has been my whole life. Working there has given me purpose and satisfaction. Now it's all going away."

"Can you change your mind about selling it?" Sarah asked, giving her a concerned look.

"Not really," said Ellie. She knew selling the Inn was a wise thing to do. She didn't want to interfere with her granddaughters' lives, and she realized more than ever that she and John needed to put money aside for future health care needs.

"How's it working out with John at home?" Liz asked.

"That's another thing I've been struggling with," Ellie said. "He's driving me crazy. He wants to cook all the time, which messes up the kitchen, or he's asking me what I'm going to do, and when I tell him, he suggests that he do it with me."

"It'll get better, but, Ellie, you have to let him have his hobbies, and then you can have time to yourself. Otherwise, he'll end up doing nothing, and that's even worse," said Liz.

"My Sam has his office. Heaven knows what he does in there, mostly reading, I guess. But he needs his space too. Does John like golf?"

"Yes, but he never took it up seriously because we were always so busy with the Inn. But maybe he'll start now. That would be great, get him out of the house, and give him some exercise."

"Ed loves to play golf," said Pat. "I'll have him give John a call."

"Thanks," said Ellie. "I guess I'm feeling sorry for myself. But I never thought I'd be so old, you know?"

"Girlfriend, we're your same age," said Liz. "You just haven't found your groove yet. You will."

Karen raised her wine glass. "Here's to us old broads. Nothing can stop us from enjoying life."

Tears stung Ellie's eyes as she lifted her glass. She loved these women.

CHAPTER FORTY

LIVY

Sitting on Austin's porch cuddled up next to him in the dark, Livy explained her concerns to him about her grandparents and the upcoming family gathering. He listened and then said, "Let's take some time off and go to South Beach to relax and have fun. It's a crazy, exciting place."

She turned to him with a smile. "You always know the right thing to say. That would be fabulous. I can't wait to have a beach break, eat delicious food, and sleep in."

"I don't know how much sleep you should plan on getting," he teased, giving her a wink.

Livy laughed. "Let me check with Brooke and Charlie to see if they'll cover for me. The day after next is my morning off, and Billy Bob is already scheduled to help."

"Sounds like a plan. Right now, let's go inside and practice," Austin said, giving her a sexy smile.

She loved it when he teased her like this.

They walked inside to his bedroom, bypassing construction that had already started in the kitchen. Livy didn't mind the mess because she loved the plans for the renovation. As she'd told Charlotte and Brooke, she liked the idea that while it would have every convenience, the completed house wouldn't be ostentatious.

Standing beside the bed, a momentary flicker of a memory with Wayne entered her mind and quickly escaped as Austin cupped her face in her hands and gave her a gentle smile. "It's okay. We'll take it slow like you want."

Sighing with happiness, Livy began to show him how much

she trusted him, how much she loved him.

Later, lying beside him, they talked about the future. She asked him if he minded that she hadn't made some crucial decisions about her work.

"I figure everything will unfold as it's supposed to. If I didn't believe that I would never have ended up with you. You're perfect for me."

"But I wish I knew what the future held. This being in limbo is driving me straight up the wall. I'm a planner, and it's hard not to know when the Inn is going to be sold or to whom. I know it's bothering Gran because she told me so. The other day, Brooke said she's pretty sure something's going on because Jake quickly ended a call as soon as he saw her walk into the office."

"Let's just enjoy time together. I'm putting a project on a hold until we know better how things are going to work out. I can set up business pretty much anywhere I want."

"I just want to be with you," said Livy, realizing she'd never said anything like it to a man. She'd follow Austin anywhere.

"You *are* with me," said Austin, pulling her close. "And I like it."

Two days later, Livy was enjoying herself by the pool at the W South Beach. Livy liked the fact that of all the hotels Austin could have chosen, he hadn't elected to stay at the biggest. The upscale property was beautiful and within a short walk from the white sandy beach. More importantly, though the hotel had every convenience, and delicious meals could be enjoyed there, it was surrounded by excellent bars and restaurants within easy walking distance.

"Enjoying yourself?" Austin asked, coming to sit beside her.

"I'm totally relaxed. I hadn't realized how stressed out I was. A nice meal tonight and a lazy morning, and I'll be ready to go back to the real world after two days of this."

"What about the spa? You told me you'd made an appointment for a massage."

Livy stretched and groaned with pleasure. "Yes, that too. Three o'clock. In time to get ready for a night of tapas so I can see what other hotels are doing with their food offerings."

Austin lay down in a chaise lounge beside her. "I could get used to this."

Livy laughed. "I know you too well. You'd end up getting bored and would want to work on a new computer program idea."

He joined her laughter. "Guess I can't fool you. But it's good to have a couple of days off."

Later, after she'd had a massage and was dressed for the evening, she and Austin strolled hand-in-hand down Ocean Drive, Collins Avenue and Lincoln Road, checking out hotels, bars, and restaurants. They stuck to their idea of light tastes of food. Livy's mind was spinning with new ideas for the Inn when she remembered there might not be much opportunity for her to use them.

The next morning, Livy awoke in their corner suite and gazed out the windows at the bright sunshine. She could see people strolling on the beach and emitted a sigh of contentment. She'd take a walk later. For now, she was enjoying the chance to lounge in bed with the man she loved.

Lying there, she wondered what life with him would be like. Though he had no pressure to be working, she knew it was what he enjoyed. She wanted children but didn't want to rush into having them. She thought of Skye and her little dachshund she'd named Bro for brother. Maybe she and Austin could start their family life with a dog.

"You're smiling," said Austin opening his eyes and looking at her.

"I was just thinking we might want to get a dog," said Livy.

"Are you talking about one like Skye's little puppy?" said Austin. "We might want something bigger."

"Or maybe two. One for me and one for you," said Livy, grinning at him.

"Whatever makes you happy," said Austin. "I could never have a dog growing up. Much too messy for my mother."

"All the more reason to get one," said Livy and they laughed together. When the time came, they'd consider it.

Later, they sat on the wraparound balcony eating breakfast ordered from room service. It was one of the most beautiful mornings Livy could ever remember. She loved being waited on, loved food, and loved the man sitting opposite her. She couldn't help lifting her face and saying a quiet thank you to the skies above them.

"Everything all right?" Austin asked.

"Perfect," she replied, feeling it to her bones.

They took a walk on the beach. Too soon, it was time to check out and return to the Gulf Coast.

On the drive home, Brooke called. "Hi, hope you had a nice break because we unexpectedly have booked a group of twelve rooms for this weekend. They arrive tomorrow."

Livy shook her head, already feeling as if the beach break was too short. "No worries. We'll handle it. Any more news about a sale?"

"No, but I'm pretty sure Jake is talking to someone about it. Believe me, right after I find out, you'll be the first to know."

After Livy ended the call, Austin reached over and squeezed her hand. “Back to work, huh?”

She nodded, more certain than ever that, going forward, she wanted to do something on her own, maybe wedding cakes, maybe a little selective catering. Not a full-time job.

The next day, as promised, the weekend group started to arrive. Livy noticed as they checked in that they all looked about the same age. When Charlotte asked, one of the women explained that they lived in the same inland neighborhood and decided to take a break at the beach. Listening to them talk about how their children played together, she wondered if she and Austin would eventually want to live in a neighborhood like that.

After getting settled in their rooms, the group gathered on the beach. A few began to play volleyball. One of the men, who'd rented a boat, brought it to the dock and tied it up there. A couple of the women went shelling even though the best hours for doing that were in the early morning.

While the group was busy with activities outside, Livy and Billy Bob worked together to create an easy meal for the dinner the guests had requested. A choice of roasted chicken or grilled steak, accompanied by salads and side dishes had been suggested. For dessert, Livy would serve a selection of her cupcakes with a choice of ice cream.

This dinner was just the kind of thing Livy had envisioned doing if the Inn remained in the family—meals that were delicious, but easy and wholesome.

John arrived in the kitchen as they were cooking. “Had to see what you were up to. You're here later than usual.”

Livy explained what they were doing. “It's something I thought would be a draw for groups. The ability to have a meal here, especially after a day of travel can be a big plus. Not that I'd want to have to cook dinner every night."

"Understood," said John. "After being in the restaurant business for many years, I was happy to give that up." He nudged Billy Bob. "Besides, that would mean I'd have to teach this big lug how to really cook."

John and Billy Bob laughed together. Livy respected John for taking a chance on Billy Bob upon his release from prison. It had worked out well.

After sitting at the kitchen table, John said, "Go ahead with what you're doing. I won't interfere. I promise."

Livy and Billy Bob looked at one another and rolled their eyes. But they understood how bored John was as he gamely remained silent.

Later that night, Livy and her cousins helped oversee the staff serving dinner. Holly was proving to be a valuable addition to the Sanderling Cove Inn team. The people who worked under her supervision loved her, and though she was a perfectionist, she made the work look easy.

After a successful dinner, Livy said goodnight to her cousins and left them in charge of closing. She'd be up early to handle the breakfast run alone. Billy Bob was taking a well-earned day off.

As she was leaving the building, it began to sprinkle and then sheets of rain suddenly fell in typical, sub-tropical fashion. Caught, Livy blindly ran to Gran's house. Soaked to the skin, she hurried inside, grabbed a clean beach towel from the laundry room, and stripped down. Covered with the towel, she put her clothes in the washer and made her way upstairs, careful not to disturb Gran and John. The wind had picked up and the fronds of the palm trees frantically waved outside her window as if calling for help.

She dried her hair, slipped on a nightshirt, and crawled into bed. Lying alone, she hugged her pillow, missing Austin. What a strange courtship it had been. But throughout it all, even Aynsley's outlandish claims, she'd understood that Austin was a good man.

Sometime during the night, the electricity went out and Livy woke to see her digital clock flashing on her bedside table. She checked the clock on her phone and jumped out of bed. She was late. And Billy Bob was off.

She got dressed, knocked on Charlotte's door, and hearing no answer dashed downstairs.

Outside, the yard was strewn with leaves, a couple of palm fronds, and twigs. Hibiscus blossoms in the landscaping around the Inn drooped, looking as if they were ashamed to lift their heads.

She hurried inside to find the kitchen dark. She snapped on the lights, grateful when they came on. Hearing voices in the breakfast room, she went to investigate. One of the women in the group of twenty-four had made coffee and she and another woman were sitting at the table talking.

"'Morning," said Livy brightly. "I'm sorry I overslept. I see you made coffee. Let me get you juice and a few nibbles to tide you over until breakfast."

"Thanks. It was pleasant to be able to sit here quietly," said the woman who Livy remembered was Jennifer.

"Well, I won't disturb you," said Livy. "Have you heard a weather report?"

"I have," said the other woman. "Last night's storm was totally unexpected, but today's forecast for showers was predicted. I was wondering if you have card tables. We can set up a bridge tournament."

"We do have a few card tables and plenty of chairs," said

Livy, grateful Brooke had pushed hard to add to the supply of them.

"Not everyone will play cards. The men said no matter what, they were going fishing," said Jennifer. "Several women in the group will opt to go shopping, but by afternoon they'll want to play cards."

"That works," said Livy. She strode into the kitchen to set out their typical early morning fare for guests. Moments after she'd laid out the coffee, juices, and goodies, Charlotte arrived.

"Sorry I'm late. Guess we lost some electricity. Crazy storm last night."

"I slept through it," Livy confessed. "Want to help me in the kitchen? It's Billy Bob's day off."

"Me?" said Charlotte laughing. "I'm not a great cook."

"Don't worry. I'll tell you exactly what to do. First of all, we need to print out orders and see what we need to get ready. I'm pretty sure bacon will be on the list."

"Okay. I can do that. I'm really going to try to learn to cook. It was so easy to eat out in New York. In fact, I want to take a cooking lesson if you'll be doing any in the future."

"We'll see. Things are still unsettled for me. But I like the idea of being able to do something like that."

As they were talking, Jake appeared with an older man. "Ah, just the people I wanted to see. I'd like to introduce David Norris to you. He's the agent representing a potential buyer for the Inn. He has permission to inspect the entire property including the plumbing, heating and cooling systems, inventory in the kitchen and elsewhere, and any areas of the property he requests to see. I saw Brooke as she was arriving, and she said you have a couple of empty guest rooms available to show him."

"Yes," said Charlotte. She held out her hand. "Hello, I'm

Charlotte Bradford. And this is my cousin, Livy Winters. I guess you've already met Brooke."

David shook her hand with a pleasant smile. "I'll try to stay out of your way, but I've promised to make a thorough inspection."

"May I ask who your client is?" Livy said.

Both Jake and David shook their heads.

"It's confidential," said Jake. "That's the way we're going to keep it."

"Okay," said Livy. "But I have to assume the buyer is serious."

"You would be right," said David.

"Livy is going to be working in the kitchen, but I'll be glad to show you around," said Charlotte.

Jake gave her a satisfied look. "That would be great, Charlie."

They left the kitchen as the regular kitchen staff arrived. "Just in time," said Livy. "Let's get busy. We've got some meals coming up in a few minutes."

Like an orchestra conductor, Livy directed people to different stations and continued printing off the list of orders.

The Inn soon filled with the sound of conversation as people appeared for breakfast and lounged in the gathering room, getting ready for the day.

The rain had stopped. The outdoors seemed to glisten from the sun's rays on rain drops that lingered on the leaves of the bushes on the property. Livy took it as an omen that the day and plans going forward would be okay. She was immediately proved wrong. After breakfast, one of the guests slipped and fell in the pool area. The woman suffered only a scrape on her knee, but a series of minor mishaps followed, including the breaking of a favorite serving bowl when David inspected the interior of the sideboard in the breakfast room.

Feeling grumpy, tired, and worried, Livy left after breakfast and decided to walk along the beach. The Gulf waters were stirred up by the storm, and it was an excellent time to go searching for shell treasures. Anything to take her mind off the business. She hadn't realized how awful she'd feel about having a representative for a new owner poking around.

She was walking along the beach when Mimi and Skye waved to her. A dachshund puppy pranced at Skye's feet and then kept up with her as Skye raced to Livy.

"Hi, Livy. Look what I found." She held up a perfect Murex shell, it's spiny surface intact.

"It's beautiful," gushed Livy, kneeling to pet the dog. "How's Bro doing?"

"He's sometimes naughty, but Mimi and I are teaching him to be a good boy." Skye patted Bro on the head, and he wiggled with enthusiasm.

Livy stood to greet Mimi. "'Morning."

Mimi smiled at her. "It looks like it might clear later. Right now, it's perfect for shelling. How are things at the Inn?"

"Gran has a prospective buyer, but we're not allowed to know who it is," said Livy. "It has put me into a tailspin."

"Change can be good, Livy. Think how this summer has changed you and the other kids."

"You're right. Guess I'm still wondering how this will affect my future."

"Well, you have a wonderful man in Austin. You'll figure it out." Mimi turned to Bro. "You stay off."

Bro gazed up at her, wagged his tail, and jumped onto her leg again.

"You little rascal," Mimi said, laughing and picking him up. "He's so adorable I can hardly scold him."

"Austin and I might get a dog," Livy said, excited by the idea.

"This one's a cutie and cuddly with Skye. It's been great for her." She turned to Skye. "C'mon, we have to get back to the house. See you later, Livy."

After they left, Livy continued on her walk feeling better. Change didn't have to be bad, did it?

CHAPTER FORTY-ONE

LIVY

The next day, Livy and her cousins sat in the office going over the schedule for the coming ten days. The family party would officially be under way in five days, but several family members were arriving early, including Livy's parents and her two brothers. Brooke's mother and fiancé would also arrive early, and Brooke was both excited and worried. Charlotte's parents would arrive by private jet on Friday, the first day of the family weekend.

Livy knew her mother was anxious to spend some time with Austin and to discuss wedding plans with her. She just hoped her mother would understand that any wedding discussions would include Austin's input. He had no desire for a big, fancy to-do. He'd already told Livy that would remind him of his mother and the way she'd always wanted things, and he wanted no part of an ostentatious event. Livy was more than fine with that.

After being here this summer, both of her cousins felt the same way about weddings of their own. The simpler the ceremonies, the more meaningful they seemed to be. The weddings at the Inn had proven it to them.

Livy worked in the kitchen to prepare and freeze cookies, cupcakes without icing, and various appetizers so they'd have plenty of backup if they needed it during that busy time.

The day before her family was due to arrive, Livy was surprised when Gran approached her and asked if she'd do her hair.

"I just need to have it cut and styled a bit," Gran said,

patting her gray hair. "After seeing women in Europe always looking well put together, I've decided I want to change my look a bit for the family weekend."

"Sure, I can do that for you," said Livy, pleased by the idea. She grinned. "Maybe we could put a streak of pink in your hair. That will make it seem more like you."

Gran's eyes lit. "Okay. Let's do it." She brushed a speck off her yellow T-shirt that said, "*Later, Gator*". "Maybe Charlie will help me pick out a suitable dress or two."

Livy hid her surprise. "She'd be perfect at that."

"Thanks, darling. Shall we plan on doing this mid-day?"

"That's doable. I'll see if Brooke wants a trim too."

Hairdressing was a far cry from baking, but both gave Livy the feeling of helping someone, and she enjoyed that.

That afternoon, Livy's bedroom turned into a salon of sorts with Gran and her two cousins sitting and chatting while Livy tended to their hair.

"That pink is going to look fantastic, Gran," said Brooke, patting her purple hair. She'd decided to keep it purple for the foreseeable future.

"I can't go all formal and regular," Gran said, beaming at the three of them. The lock of hair wrapped in foil shined above her brow.

Charlotte's trim of her long auburn hair was easily done. Brooke just needed a trim of her bangs. Rather than leaving, they stayed in the room eager to see what haircut Livy would come up with for Gran.

Once Gran's hair was shampooed and ready, Livy turned to her cousins. "I'm thinking of a soft pixie, not too short. Thoughts?"

"Lovely. Not too short, though," said Charlotte.

"I agree," said Brooke.

Gran drew a deep breath and let it out. She'd been wearing her hair short in a sort of bob that she didn't do much with. "Okay, I trusted you three to run my Inn for the summer. I guess I can trust you to come up with a new idea for my hair."

Livy hid her nervousness and reminded herself she'd done this sort of thing for a couple of years. Brooke loved the haircut Livy had given her. Gran would love hers too.

Working steadily, Livy snipped, combed, and shaped. When she finally finished and stood back to study it, she knew she'd been right all along. But she hadn't been prepared for the change in Gran. She looked fifteen years younger.

"Wow," gushed Brooke.

"Fabulous," Charlotte said. "I'll put a little makeup on you. Then, you'll be set."

"Makeup? I don't want to give John another heart attack," joked Gran, gazing at herself in Livy's hand mirror with a smile. She turned to Livy. "Thank you. I love it. You are so talented."

"You're welcome. I'm happy I could do this for you. Now I have to give myself a little trim."

Later, Livy watched Gran talking to guests and realized what an attractive woman she was, always ready with a smile and a kind word.

When she saw the way John's gaze remained on Gran, she knew she'd done an excellent job.

Livy was working alone in the kitchen the next day when Gran walked in, her face flushed, her eyes sparkling. "I need your help. But this must remain confidential. A secret wedding is to take place here over the family weekend. I need you to be prepared to make the cake and a few other items, keeping the details to yourself."

"Jo and Chet are getting married here? How sweet," said Livy, excited by the idea.

"Sssh. No one is to know anything about a wedding. Not until the last moment."

"I promise not to say a word to anyone."

Two days later, Livy raced out of the Inn to greet her parents and brothers. They'd called to say they were almost at the cove.

Seeing them in their rented car waving at her with big smiles on their faces, tears stung Livy's eyes. She hadn't realized how much she'd missed them. She'd always felt close to her father. Jack Winters had insisted on adopting her soon after his marriage to her mother. And her brothers? They were babies she welcomed as much as her parents. Now, Hunter at fourteen and Jason at sixteen were handsome, healthy boys who loved sports.

"Hi, sis," Hunter called. He and his brother jumped out of the car and gave her hugs.

"You've grown," Livy said to her brothers, stretching on her toes to give each one a kiss.

"Can't wait to get into the pool," said Hunter.

"I'm off to the beach," cried Jason, sprinting away.

Hunter followed his older brother as he had from his time as a toddler.

Livy laughed and turned as her mother hurried toward her, arms outstretched.

Her mother was not much larger than she. Natural blonde hair, blue eyes, a cute figure, and a sparkling personality continued to serve her well. She had many friends and was involved in a lot of activities. Livy knew that Gran's first husband had doted on Leigh and understood why. Her mother was so alive. Maybe that was the same reason Livy had sometimes felt diminished by her mother's presence.

Livy hugged her, happy to see her. Though they disagreed on some things, their bond was strong. For a while, after her mother had been ditched by the boyfriend who'd gotten her pregnant, it had been just the two of them until Leigh fell for her boss, Jack. That was a happy marriage for all.

Livy kissed her father. "Hi, Dad. I'm glad you're here. I've told Austin how smart you are as a financial advisor, and he may want to talk business with you."

"I'd be happy to talk to him, but we're here to help you two celebrate your engagement and to be with the others for a special family weekend. You're what's important." He gave her an extra squeeze.

"Is anyone else here from the family yet?" her mother asked.

Livy shook her head. "Brooke's mom and her fiancé come tomorrow. Aunt Vanessa and Uncle Walter will arrive on Friday."

"Oh, that will give Jo and me each some private time with Gran. Where is she?"

"Here I am, Leigh," said Gran rounding the corner of the Inn. In place of her usual T-shirt, she was wearing a pretty pink knit top that Charlotte had helped her pick out.

"Mom, you look fabulous!" cried Leigh, hurrying forward to embrace her. "What's that pink in your hair?"

"A subtle sign of defiance," Gran said with a smile of satisfaction.

"Guess having all the girls together has been marvelous in many ways," said Livy's mother, hugging her.

"That and a honeymoon," said Gran. John appeared and placed an arm around her shoulder.

"Glad to see you," said John. He grinned even harder when her mother gave him a big hug. "Congratulations to both you and Mom. It's nice that it's official."

"Shacking up was pretty nice, too," said Gran unable to prevent goading her daughter.

"A wedding was long overdue," sighed her mother.

Livy knew it had bothered her that Gran and John had lived together for years without marrying. "Wait until you hear all about the honeymoon trip," she said, hoping to ease the brief moment of unease.

"I'm anxious to hear about all the places you visited. We all enjoyed your photos online." Her mother smiled at Gran and John. "What a special time the two of you must have had." She wrapped an arm around Livy. "It certainly has been a fantastic summer for Livy and her cousins. Such happy news everywhere."

"I still can't believe Austin and I are engaged," said Livy shyly.

"Life sure is full of surprises, especially when I remember you had a crush on him as a teenager," said her mother.

"I still do," Livy said, and they all laughed. "Come on inside. Your rooms are ready for you. I can't wait to show you more of the changes we made. They're subtle but appealing."

"I already noticed the new sign out front. Very classy," said her father. "And I liked the new PR materials Charlie put together."

"Speaking of Charlie," said Livy. "Here she is now."

Charlotte joined them. "Hi, Aunt Leigh. Uncle Jack." Charlotte embraced them both. "We're glad you're here to start off the weekend."

"Congratulations on your engagement," her mother said. "I think it's wonderful that you and Livy will be sisters-in-law. That makes it unique and special."

"Yes, we've already talked about it," said Charlotte with a teasing twinkle in her eye. "Being married to the oldest Ensley man, I will be able to dictate how family things are to be done."

Charlotte and Livy laughed. They were both well aware that among the three cousins no one was in charge.

"I was just going to take my parents inside and show them some of the things we worked on this summer. Want to join us?" asked Livy. "Is Brooke inside?"

"Yes, I'll come with you. Brooke is in the office."

"Perfect," said Livy.

"John and I will meet you later," said Gran. "Enjoy the tour. I'll go check on the boys. Guess they couldn't wait to get their toes into the sand. Following that, John and I have a meeting to attend."

Livy, Charlotte, and her parents entered the Inn. As Livy was showing her parents the breakfast room, Brooke appeared.

"Hi, Aunt Leigh and Uncle Jack. Welcome to the Inn." She gave them each a hug. "I hope you like the changes we made."

"So far, I see a big improvement," said Livy's mother. "As Livy said, they're subtle but meaningful, with many little things being done for a new, improved look."

"You girls must have worked hard," said her father.

"We didn't want to let Gran and John down," Brooke said. "I can't wait for my mother to see everything."

"Well, I can't wait to see *her*," said Leigh. "It's such thrilling news to know she's happy and in love. Her life has been a struggle from time to time."

"Yes," said Brooke. "She seems like a totally different person."

"And you're in love, too," said Livy's mother. "I'm very

happy for all of you."

"I don't know if you remember Dylan, but he's a successful artist now. I'm helping him by assisting with the galleries who show his work."

"How delightful. It will be great to catch up with everyone." Livy's mother turned to her. "Let's see what else you've done."

After completing the tour and ushering her parents to their rooms, Livy heaved a silent sigh of relief.

She joined Brooke and Charlotte in the office. "I think my mother approves of what we've done."

"She certainly did," said Charlotte. "And your dad thought it was great to have done this before the sale."

Livy sighed. "I still can't believe the Inn is being sold. Brooke, any news about the secret buyer?"

Brooke shook her head. "Not a word, though Jake had to cancel a meeting with me because he's working on the sale. When I asked if he could give me a hint about it, he shut me down quickly."

"Well, I hope whoever's interested in the Inn respects the property for what it is—a charming place to escape to with excellent facilities and service," said Charlotte.

"Me, too," said Livy. "See you later. Austin is meeting me here in a few minutes so we can meet with my parents."

"Good luck," said Brooke.

Livy left them and went outside to wait for Austin. She wasn't nervous about him talking with her parents, just hopeful that they'd both understand about any non-traditional wedding plans.

The minute she saw Austin drive into the parking lot, she felt the tension leave her. She and Austin loved and trusted one another, no matter how long wedding plans were put off.

"Hey," Austin said, exposing his adorable dimple as he smiled at her.

She eagerly went into his arms. "I can't wait for my parents to get to know you. Come on. We're going to meet them in their room and talk on the patio."

Her father opened the door to his room and beaming, shook hands with Austin. Her mother approached, and pausing for only a second, swept Austin into a hug. Seeing the look of delight on his face, Livy sent a silent thank you to her mother. After living with a cold mother who could be cruel at times, a warm hug was exactly the right way to greet Austin.

"Come inside. I've set up some refreshments on the patio. I thought we could sit and talk there where we have privacy."

"Great," said Austin, following her parents outside.

They all took seats, and then after a bit of small talk, Austin told Livy's father about the business he'd sold and some other opportunities he was looking into.

While the men talked, Livy's mother signaled for her to come inside. "Time for girl talk. I haven't taken a close look at your ring. Austin mentioned he designed it. That makes it extra special."

Livy held out her left hand. She found it hard to believe that the huge diamond was hers. But like her mother said, she'd wear it in honor of Austin and their love, not hide it in a safe deposit box.

"I have some ideas for weddings and dresses. I was talking to Maribelle the other day and she mentioned a new designer she'd heard about."

Livy held up a hand to stop her. "Mom, I don't want to hurt your feelings, but both Austin and I want to be married here at the Inn or somewhere else on the coast in a beach wedding with a small number of family and friends."

"Oh, honey, are you sure? I have some ideas, and my friends would love to see you married ..." She stopped talking as Livy's frown deepened. "We can decide all this later."

Livy remained silent. She wanted a small intimate wedding and wouldn't change her mind. Maybe in time, being here in the cove, her mother would understand.

CHAPTER FORTY-TWO

BROOKE

Brooke stood in the baggage claim area at the Tampa International Airport as planned, waiting for her mother and Chet to arrive. She sometimes felt she no longer knew the woman who'd been her mother, that a happy-go-lucky stranger had taken her place. But when she saw her familiar form cross the floor toward her, Brooke sprinted forward to give her a hug.

Chet smiled at them. Of average height and build, and wearing glasses, Chet's hazel eyes and expression radiated a peaceful kindness as he held out his hand for her to shake.

"Hi, Brooke. It's a pleasure to meet you in person, though I feel as if I already know you, between what your mother has said about you and our phone calls."

"I can't tell you how happy I am for both of you." She was caught off guard by unexpected tears. "You make my mother so happy."

"As she does me," he said softly, giving Brooke's hand a brief squeeze before he wrapped an arm around her mother's shoulders. "Jo and I are a good team."

The loving looks they shared meant so much to Brooke. She knew exactly how they felt because that's what she and Dylan shared.

"Let's get your bags, and we'll head right to the cove where you can relax. I'm sure Livy has prepared something delicious for lunch."

"It's terrific that you three women have been able to work this well together," said her mother. "How fabulous that Mom and John were able to enjoy an entire summer in Europe because of you." She stood back and studied Brooke. "You look beautiful. So happy."

Brooke held out her left hand. "It's sometimes hard for me to believe I'm engaged. It happened quickly, but I know it's right. Dylan's the best thing that's ever happened to me. We'll all have lunch together to get to know one another better."

"I already like what I see in Dylan, but lunch together sounds great," her mother said.

As they made their way toward the baggage belt, Brooke noticed that her mother walked briskly with no apparent pain. Amazing what love and attention could do, she thought. Watching her mother and Chet together, Brooke was more than a little grateful to Chet. He'd changed her life as well as her mother's.

At the cove, a crowd gathered around them after they drove into the parking lot. Brooke had phoned ahead and was grateful to see many members of the family there to greet them.

Gran and John hugged Brooke, shook hands with Chet, and stood back as other members of the family took their turns. Brooke observed Aunt Leigh and her mother embrace with interest. The sisters were so different.

Livy spoke. "Okay, everyone, I've prepared a special luncheon. Billy Bob and I will serve from the kitchen, and we can eat together in the private dining room."

Brooke took hold of her mother's arm. "I'll show you and Chet all around the Inn after lunch."

"That would be spectacular. While I'm here I also want to have some time alone with you."

"Perfect."

Dylan and Austin showed up together. More introductions were made and then they moved inside.

After picking up their food in the kitchen, everyone moved to the dining room where they could sit and talk away from other guests in the house.

Brooke and her mother had often been alone for holidays and other occasions when family was important because of Jo's unwillingness to travel. Now, sitting in this room with everyone, Brooke's heart warmed. This is what she wanted for the family she and Dylan would have someday.

John entertained the group with stories from their trip, adding details to those he'd spoken of earlier. It was a superb way to make everyone feel comfortable.

Aunt Leigh and her mother were sitting next to each other, chatting privately and laughing. Brooke could well imagine them as children. Aunt Leigh the bubbly outgoing girl; her mother, the quiet, studious one. It made Brooke realize how beneficial the summer had been, breaking away from old patterns, discovering new things about herself.

Chet seemed to understand what she was thinking and gave her a wink. "Good to see your mother like this, huh?"

Brooke beamed at him. "It's wonderful. I know that as long as she's with you, I won't have to worry about her."

"She's quite a remarkable woman," he said. "Much stronger than many imagined."

Brooke glanced at her mother, who was now talking with Dylan. So many changes from a summer at Sanderling Cove.

After lunch, Charlotte joined her in giving a tour to Brooke's mother and Chet.

"Very impressive," her mother told them. She turned to Chet. "It's always been an attractive place, but it needed a little dressing up. Too bad the Inn is for sale. I have such torn feelings about it. Mom and John deserve a break, but the Inn has been part of our lives for a long time. Not just for our family, but for the families here at the cove. I'm sure they have mixed feelings too."

"Yes," said Charlotte. "It's a sad thing for all the families. They don't like the idea of the Inn being run by outsiders."

Later, after her mother had taken a well-deserved nap, they headed down to the beach.

Brooke slung an arm around her mother's shoulder. "I'm glad we could have this time together. I want you to know how truly happy I am that you've found a man like Chet. There's something very special about him. And I see how much he cares for you."

Her mother beamed at her. "I feel as if my whole life is just beginning. All those years alone weren't easy for either of us. I know there were times when you missed having a father present. I'm just sorry it took me so long to find a man I could love."

Her mother stopped and faced her. Tears escaped from behind her sunglasses. "Oh, Brookie, I've realized how much of your own life you've given up for me. Will you forgive me?"

Brooke hugged her hard. "Of course. It's worked both ways. You've always been there for me, Mom. I love you."

Her mother sniffed and patted a tissue to her eyes. "Dylan adores you. That makes me happy. You deserve that. What a life together you two will have."

Brooke gave her a steady look. "We'll visit often, but I'm never really coming home again."

Her mother laughed. "I know that. The world is your home now. Chet and I have already talked about buying a new house. A fresh start for both of us. But we'll always have room for you and Dylan and any grandchildren that may come."

"Children won't be for a while, but we want at least three or four."

"Marvelous, darling. Marvelous."

They stood and hugged each other, thankful for all they'd been given.

CHAPTER FORTY-THREE

CHARLOTTE

Charlotte waited in the office for a call from her mother. They'd agreed to meet outside the Inn. Her parents had flown into St. Petersburg-Clearwater International Airport in a private jet and had hired a limo to bring them to the Inn. A little ostentatious, but that's the kind of service they were used to. And Walter, her stepfather, was a busy man.

Although he didn't often have time for her, Charlotte respected and loved Walter. He hadn't legally adopted her, but he treated her as his own daughter. With no siblings to vie for his attention, it had worked out well. He was a quiet supporter of hers when tension grew between her and her mother.

Charlotte sighed. Her mother was a hard act to follow. Stunningly beautiful, well spoken, determined to be seen and heard, she would've made a great politician except for the fact that she didn't easily suffer fools. But this same presence had brought about a lot of goodwill from the charities in which she participated.

Charlotte had no qualms about Shane meeting her. His own mother had an unmistakable presence. But the difference between the women was striking. Whereas Diana had been insecure and cruel at times, her own mother was sure-footed and kind.

At last, the call came.

Charlotte went outside to greet them. She waited for the driver to open the door and watched as her mother emerged, one wedge-sandaled foot after the other. A smile lit her beautiful face as she stood. "Hi, darling. I'm so happy to see you."

They met halfway, and Charlotte leaned in for a hug. She realized she'd missed speaking to her mother in person. Phone conversations were not enough.

"You look wonderful, Charlotte," her mother said. "Love looks good on you."

"I can't wait for you to spend some time with Shane. I know from earlier conversations that you want to discuss the Family First program with him."

"Yes, I do. It seems like a fabulous opportunity for young people. Something I might be interested in." She turned and smiled at Walter, who approached with his arms open.

Charlotte hurried into them.

"Hi, sweet girl. It's wonderful to see you. I can't wait to personally meet the man you've chosen to marry. I've talked to him, of course, and seen his picture." He looked up and grinned. "Here he is now."

The two men greeted each other, shook hands, and then Shane faced her mother with a broad smile. "Hello, Mrs. Van Pelt. I'm pleased to meet you." He placed an arm around Charlotte. "I love your daughter."

"I do too," said her mother. "And, please, Shane, call me Vanessa. We're going to be family."

He chuckled. "Thanks."

"Come inside. Your rooms are ready," said Charlotte. "Welcome to the Sanderling Cove Inn. I can't wait to show you some changes since you were here last."

"Charlie and her cousins have done a great job refreshing the place," said Shane.

"It will be a relief to have it off my mother's hands. And John's too, of course," said her mother. "I worry about the two of them working so hard at their ages."

"We're all quite sad about the sale of it. All the cove families are," said Charlotte.

"I too will be sorry to see it go, but it's been a worry these last few years. But, come, let's see what the summer has brought to it."

"I'll get your luggage," said Shane. He grabbed their two small suitcases and followed them inside.

Charlotte gave a tour to her parents, listening carefully to their comments. Pleased that they liked the improvements, Charlotte said, "It's a perfect place for weddings. We've put on a few."

Her mother gave her a sharp look but remained quiet.

Shane spoke up. "We're thinking of a beach wedding right here at the cove."

This time her mother couldn't restrain herself. "A nice idea for others, but not for you. We have many friends who want to be part of her special day ... your special day. There are many possibilities of something a little more ... upscale in New York."

"Now is not the time to discuss this, dear," said Walter gently.

She glanced at him. "Okay. Let's get settled in our room. Cocktail time is five o'clock. Right, Charlotte?"

"Yes, and then Granny Liz is having us all to a beach party. Tomorrow, we're having a more formal dinner in the dining room here at the Inn."

"Oh, my! One of Liz's beach parties. Does that bring back a few memories." Her mother turned to Walter. "You would've loved them. Lots of sailing back then."

"Sailing has played an important role in Shane and me discovering each other," said Charlotte grinning at him.

Shane. "My mermaid. We'll tell you the story later."

"Sounds intriguing," her mother said, bringing a soft giggle from Charlotte. She loved hearing Shane talk about how she'd saved his life.

"Here's my number one daughter," came a cry behind them, and Gran rushed over to greet them, followed by John.

Her mother's eyes widened. "Mom, you look terrific! Love the sassy pink in your hair and the way it's styled." She hugged Gran, then turned to John. "Congratulations on the wedding. I was disappointed to miss it, like we all were, but I'm happy you two have made it official."

"So much easier," John said with a twinkle in his eye.

Charlotte knew he was giving her mother a gentle tease, but she didn't seem to notice.

Walter exchanged a hug with Gran and shook hands with John.

"Quite a family gathering," said Walter. "It's delightful for all of us to be together."

"Yes, everyone is here. Henry Ensley and his family. KK Hendrix and her family are here too. Seeing as how we all are to be connected, it seemed appropriate."

"Fantastic. I haven't seen anyone in so long, it's going to be great fun catching up." Her mother smiled at Gran. "I'm happy that you and John can just relax in the years to come. I'm sure we'll all get used to someone outside the family running it."

"There are a lot of changes coming," said Gran looking flustered.

"C'mon, Mom. Let's get you settled in your room, and you can relax a bit before our social hour." Charlotte glanced at the linen sheath her mother wore. "You might want to get in more comfortable clothes. You're at the beach, remember?"

Her mother laughed. "I forget how casual it is at the cove."

"As it should be," said Gran with a slight edge to her voice. "Those are the different lifestyles we've chosen."

Charlotte took Gran's arm. "Let's get them settled."

They went inside, and as they walked through the property, Charlotte pointed out some of the recent changes.

"I'd forgotten how charming this Inn could be," said her mother, gazing around with interest.

Charlotte exhaled the breath she'd been holding. Her mother's approval still meant a lot to her.

Charlotte opened the door to their suite with a flourish. She'd made sure fresh flowers, bottles of water, and a basket of snacks were in the room. The new sheets, bedspread, and pillows in the room added a fresh, colorful touch.

Walter placed a hand on Charlotte's shoulder. "Thank you. I see how nice you've made everything for us."

"There's a bottle of champagne in the refrigerator. I thought the four of us could share that later after you've had a chance to change."

"I'd better be on my way," said Shane. "I have a few business calls to make."

Her mother pulled him in for a hug.

Walter shook Shane's hand. "Glad to meet the man who's won our Charlotte's heart."

"She had me from the beginning. It just took a bang on the head to make me realize how much I loved her."

Charlotte laughed. "Part of the long story. We'll share it with you later. Hurry and get changed, and we'll meet you out on the beach. We've set up chairs and umbrellas for everyone."

"All right," said her mother. "See you two later."

Charlotte and Shane left the room.

"Your parents seem great. I vaguely remember your mother. You look a lot like her."

"Thanks," said Charlotte, taking it as a compliment.

###

Later, when her mother and Walter came to the beach, Charlotte grabbed a chair under one of the umbrellas. Her mother's fair skin burned easily, and she had to be careful of the sun. The other women in the group, understanding, came and sat there.

Charlotte took hold of Walter's arm and introduced him to Henry and Gordon Hendrix and went inside to see if she could help Liz. Beach parties had always been Granny Liz's thing, but as she aged, she welcomed more and more help.

Inside the kitchen, she was surprised to see Grace and Belinda.

Charlotte hugged them both. "I didn't know the two of you had arrived. I'm pleased you could take some time off from the restaurant to join us."

Grace and Belinda exchanged looks, then Grace said, "A problem has come up with the lease on our restaurant space so we're taking a short break."

"Oh, I'm sorry to hear that. Gills was such an enjoyable seafood restaurant."

"Things always work out for the best," said Belinda with a certainty Charlotte admired.

"I'd better go change for the guests at the Inn. Everyone is invited to join us. Please come."

"We will," said Grace. "Thanks."

Charlotte went outside, spoke to Gran, then went to Gran's house to change. She didn't mind mingling with the guests. It was an excellent way to learn something new. Tonight, would be special because she'd have a chance to talk to everyone in the family.

CHAPTER FORTY-FOUR

LIVY

As Livy circulated among hotel guests and family members attending the social hour, she felt a pang at never being able to do this again. Brooke had whispered to her that she'd finally gotten some news out of Jake about the sale of the Inn. The deal was all but closed.

Livy observed the different family members around her and noticed how her mother fit in with her older sisters. Charlotte's mother was definitely the one who was more remote, more sophisticated, more in control. Just like Charlotte. Aunt Jo was sweet and eager to see that everyone around her was happy. Brooke, too, was a caretaker. Livy's mother was the adored one in the family, secure and bubbly in her interactions.

"A penny for your thoughts," said her father.

"Just thinking what a special family we have. I want that for Austin too."

Her father put an arm on her shoulder. "You're a kind, loving person. With you, he will have that. Your mother and I are pleased to have him in the family, and we'll make sure he knows we welcome him."

"I know, but Mom wants the kind of wedding we don't want," said Livy.

"Let your mother fuss over an engagement party," her father said. "I'll take care of the rest."

Livy turned and hugged him hard.

Austin approached them. "Nice party, huh?"

"Very much so," said Livy's father. "I'll leave you two, but,

Austin, I'm glad we'll have a chance tomorrow to discuss those ideas you have about a new business."

After her father walked away, Austin said, "I like your family."

"I'm glad you'll be a part of it." Livy squeezed his hand. "In fact, you already are."

Charlotte waved to them. "C'mon, you two. Gran has an announcement to make. We're meeting in the private dining room."

Curious, Livy and Austin followed the others inside the room. A table to the side of the room displayed two silver buckets holding ice and green wine bottles. Tulip glasses for champagne lined up next to them.

Livy's excitement grew. She was certain Aunt Jo and Chet's wedding was about to be announced.

Gran and John faced the family and members of the cove family who'd gathered round them.

"We have an important announcement," said Gran smiling, though her eyes were shiny with tears. "We've sold The Sanderling Cove Inn."

A hush fell over the group.

"It's all good news," said John.

"*Very* good news," added Gran. "We're proud and pleased to introduce you to the new owners. Grace and Belinda."

Livy clapped her hands to her face, so shocked she couldn't speak. Then she began to clap. Soon the room filled with applause.

"Perfect! Wonderful!" were just some of the cries that reverberated in the space.

Once the room had quieted, Grace spoke. "Belinda and I are very excited about this new opportunity. As some of you may know, our landlord made staying in Clearwater almost impossible with a huge increase of rent in our building. After talking it over, we decided to approach Gran and John about the possibility of running the Inn." Her voice caught. "Instead, they offered to sell it to us for a price we couldn't refuse."

Gran stepped between the couple and placed a hand on each of their shoulders. "We wanted the Inn to stay among family, and we can't think of any two people who will be better at keeping the Inn at its best. Anyone who's eaten at their restaurant knows how superb Grace and Belinda are in this business. Best of all, Amby, Beryl, Billy Bob, and other valuable members of the staff will be allowed to stay."

"We'll be making some changes, adding dinners as Livy has suggested in the past." Grace turned to her. "We're hoping you'll take part in some of those dinners. We'll talk to you about it another time."

Livy grinned. Maybe the future wasn't as uncertain as she'd thought.

"I think we all should toast Grace and Belinda and wish them well," said John. He opened one bottle of champagne and then the other, sliding the corks out with a soft pop of anticipation.

Gordon Hendrix, Grace's father, helped pour the champagne into glasses and hand them out. As soon as everyone had theirs, he raised a glass. "Here's to Grace and Belinda, a wonderful couple, a splendid team. We wish you the best going forward."

"Hear! Hear!" said John, clinking glasses with Gran.

Once everyone had toasted the couple, Gran spoke. "I know some of you are curious about the arrangements we've made. Grace and Belinda will officially take over the Inn next week. That will give them time to transition to ownership before the holiday season starts. John and I will continue to live at my house. We wanted to keep the house, so my family has the right to maintain a footprint in Sanderling Cove. It has been a happy place for our children and grandchildren."

Livy went to Grace and gave her a hug. "I'm so happy the Inn is staying in the cove family." She turned to Belinda. "You two deserve a break after working hard building a business and having it torn away from you by a greedy landlord." She nudged Belinda. "No wonder you were optimistic about the future. You already knew about the Inn."

Belinda laughed. "Yes. But I truly believe things happen for a reason. Owning this Inn, presenting dinners just a couple nights a week instead of every night will be such a relief. Running the restaurant became too much."

Livy glanced at John. He'd gladly given up his restaurant to help with the Inn.

Brooke and Charlotte joined them.

"Fabulous news," said Charlotte to Grace and Belinda. "You two are going to do great."

"The Inn will be even better than we tried to make it," Brooke said.

"We're hoping each of you stays involved to some degree," said Grace. "That's something we discussed with Gran. We don't want you to feel shut out."

"I'm happy to help from time to time," said Livy. "Maybe we can come up with a plan after you've run the Inn for a few months."

"And I can check in from time to time," Brooke said. "Do any financial matters remotely."

"I'm happy to take you on as special clients," said Charlotte.

Gran came over to them. "Ah, there are my girls. All five of you are so talented I know it will work out well."

Livy couldn't help wondering about the surprise wedding. She gave Gran a questioning look.

Gran shook her head and then walked away.

Livy hurried to catch up to her.
"What about the wedding?" she whispered in Gran's ear.
Gran gave her a cryptic smile. "Wait and see."

CHAPTER FORTY-FIVE

ELLIE

Ellie awoke early the next morning and quietly slipped out of bed. The rising sun was sending shafts of sunlight into the brightening sky. It was a perfect day for a secret wedding. With the family gathered, it made all the sense in the world for a couple to use the time for a celebration of this kind.

She slipped on a pair of shorts, a pink T-shirt that said, "*Que Sera Sera*", and her pink sparkling sandals, her favorite. An early morning walk on the beach.

As she stepped outside, Ellie inhaled the cool salty air. Living near water fulfilled something deep inside her, and living in the cove with people she loved made it even better.

She walked to the edge of lawn, kicked off her sandals and stepped onto the cool sand of the beach. Later the sand would warm, but now it was refreshing on her feet. She moved to the edge of the water and stood facing the Gulf. Behind her, sandpipers and sanderlings scurried by, leaving their footprints in the wet sand. Above her, seagulls and terns circled, riding the wind like a kite, making Ellie wish she could fly with them.

A figure approached, and she turned to see John smiling at her. "I thought I might find you here." He kissed her, sending a wave of warmth through her. He was such a dear man.

Ellie took hold of his hand and squeezed it. "Looks like it's going to be a beautiful day."

"Indeed," he said, smiling down at her. "A beautiful day for a beautiful woman."

She couldn't hide a smile of her own. He loved making statements like this.

"Gran! Gran!" came a cry.

Ellie turned and waved at Skye running toward her, her puppy at her side. Ellie and the other women of Sanderling Cove had brought their grandchildren together in hopes of adding more little ones in their lives. She held out her arms, and Skye ran into them.

"It's going to be another party day," said Skye. "Mimi told me."

"Yes, it is. When the cove families get together it's a perfect time for a party."

"I've got a new dress for it," said Skye. "It's pink. My favorite color."

"Pretty. Pink is my favorite color too."

Skye bobbed her head. "I know. You have a lot of pink things."

Ellie looked down at her T-shirt and laughed.

Skye's father, Adam, walked up to them. "Hi. Another spectacular day."

"Yes," said Ellie. "I'd better get to the Inn. We're putting together a big breakfast for everyone. Don't forget to come. There's another important announcement."

Adam gave her a little salute. "See you then."

CHAPTER FORTY-SIX

LIVY

Livy awoke and rolled over to face Austin. She loved to start her day this way, sharing the anticipation of more time with the man she loved. He opened his eyes and smiled at her.

She kissed him, inhaling the manly smell that was his alone. "Good morning."

He drew her closer. "Are you sure you have to get up right now?"

She hugged him hard and pulled away. "I promised Gran I'd help her today. She specifically asked me."

"Okay, then. I'll see you for the big breakfast." He watched Livy as she strolled across the floor heading for the shower. At the last minute, she kicked up her heel and formed a flirty pose to make him laugh.

"I like it," he said, chuckling with her.

Later, as soon as she could, she headed to the Inn. Unless plans had changed, there was going to be a wedding today. Livy could hardly wait. Jo and Chet were so cute together, and she knew Brooke would be thrilled.

At the Inn, while Livy made the cake, John and Billy Bob handled the regular guests' breakfasts and worked on breakfast items for the family.

Charlotte came into the kitchen. "We're setting up for the breakfast in the private dining room. Right?"

"Yes," said Livy. "Why?"

"Gran and Rosalie are arranging flowers there. Do you

know why?"

Livy shrugged, willing herself not to spill the beans. "Better go see what she needs. Breakfast will be served soon. Make sure everyone is there."

"Okay," said Charlotte. "Aunt Jo and Chet have already helped themselves to coffee in the Breakfast Room."

"How sweet," said Livy thinking of the day ahead for them. As soon as Charlotte left the kitchen, Livy began working on the icing and filling for the cake. Gran had told her to make a rich, yellow cake with a strawberry cream filling, white icing in a white lace pattern topped by fresh pink flowers and a few small sea shells.

After she got the icing and filling ready, it was time to go into the dining room to join the others for breakfast.

The table laden with food looked inviting. Puzzled by the lack of people in line for the breakfast buffet, Livy noticed family members standing by.

"All right," said Gran, acknowledging her, "Everyone is here. We have another announcement to make."

Livy glanced at Aunt Jo and Chet standing together.

"We have a special wedding planned for today at the Inn," continued Gran. "Please come to the gazebo at four o'clock for the ceremony." She looped her arm through John's. "Knowing some of you were disappointed by not being present earlier, John and I decided to do a second wedding ceremony here at the Inn, especially for you, our family."

The room erupted into applause, and then everyone began to speak.

Livy looked at Gran and laughed. What a trickster.

Gran came over to her. "Thanks for keeping my secret. I didn't want anyone to take away from the excitement."

"It's a terrific idea. We have a perfect day to do it. But what about dinner?"

"Grace and Belinda are catering it. This will give them a chance to test the kitchen to see what changes they might want to make to it."

"Everything is well-planned. How long ago did you decide to do this?" Livy asked.

"We were sitting in a town square in Sicily. Some of John's family are from that area. Anyway, we decided we should've had family with us for the most important day in our lives. Now, we will."

Livy hugged her. "I'll do a beautiful job with the cake."

"I hope you three musketeers will come to my bedroom before the ceremony. I have something special to give to you."

"Okay. I can fix your hair then, if you'd like."

Gran grinned. "That might be helpful. Truth be told, I'm a little nervous about appearing as a bride."

That afternoon, Livy went to Gran's bedroom as she'd requested. When she arrived, Brooke and Charlotte were already there, sitting on the edge of the bed, inspecting Gran in her dress.

Gran twirled around. "What do you think? Charlie didn't realize it at the time, but she helped me pick this out for the wedding."

"It's perfect," gushed Livy.

Gran was wearing a tea-length, capped sleeve, white sundress with a lacy border at the hem and around the scooped neckline. On one foot, she wore a sparkly, pink sandal. The other foot was encased in her walking cast on which she'd pinned some pink silk flowers.

Livy held up a few stems of the pink freesia she'd taken from one of the flower arrangements Rosalie had made for the occasion. "We'll weave some of these in a circlet to wear on your head. With your short hair, it should look great."

"Thanks. I love the idea," said Gran. "Now take a seat."

Livy sat next to Brooke on the bed. "What's going on?"

Gran handed each of them a small package wrapped in gold foil. "I wanted each of you to have something special from John and me for allowing us to have the trip of a lifetime. We knew the summer would be a challenge for you, but I never doubted you'd meet it. You're my dear, darling granddaughters."

"Should we open them now?" Brooke asked, her eyes teary.

"Yes, I want you to wear them to the wedding," Gran replied.

Livy unwrapped her present and opened the white-leather box. Inside, lay a white-gold chain with a love-knot pendant. Two entwined circles with a sparkling diamond nestled between them.

"It's called a grandmother's love-knot," said Gran. "I hope you'll wear the necklaces knowing how much I love you, how proud I am of each of you."

"It's gorgeous," said Brooke.

"Beautiful," said Charlotte holding the necklace up to the light pouring into the room. The sunlight on the diamond sent rainbows dancing around it.

Livy clasped her hand around the necklace, touched to the core. She would wear it close to her heart, remembering how this summer and her grandmother had changed her life.

Gran kissed each of them and straightened. "Okay, let's get the show on the road. I don't want John to back out."

"As if," said Charlotte laughing. But Livy noticed her eyes were glistening too.

They helped one another with the necklaces and then Brooke and Livy turned to the task of making the circlet of flowers for Gran's hair while Charlotte made up Gran's face.

As they stepped out of the room, Livy heard guitar music.

"You girls go ahead and get settled at the gazebo," said Gran. "John and I will join you there."

Livy followed her cousins outside to the gazebo. As they'd all hoped, the weather had held. The skies were like a canopy above them, their blueness broken by puffy white clouds that resembled dollops of the icing Livy had made earlier.

She went to Austin's side and took hold of his hand. As he turned to her, Livy was aware of her mother smiling at them, and she filled with satisfaction.

It was a quiet group. Even her brothers were standing still, awaiting the moment when Gran and John would appear. The bride and groom had decided to walk together to the gazebo. The minister inside the structure would speak to them there, while the family stood around the building within easy hearing distance.

The guitar player seated inside the gazebo started playing Bach's *Cello Prelude in C*, and all eyes turned to see Gran and John slowly making their way toward them.

Together they made a handsome couple. Though Gran was in her seventies, she looked much younger. Beside her John strode full of confidence, a huge smile on his face.

Livy heard several gasps in the audience and felt her eyes fill. Gran was absolutely beautiful, made more so by the look of joy on her face.

John led Gran carefully up the steps to the inside of the gazebo, stopping before the minister who stood behind the white table Adam had built for them. The pink floral arrangement on top of the table was a stunning touch to the simplicity of the setting.

The minister spoke, and when it was time for Gran and John to exchange vows even the birds in the sky seemed to know they had to be quiet.

Gran and John faced one another holding hands.

John's words were simple and direct. "I love you, Ellie. I have from the moment we met. When we became partners, my love for you added a new dimension to what we had and grew even deeper. And now on this day, being married to you in front of family, I have no words to describe the love that fills my heart except to simply say, 'I love you, Ellie Rizzo.'"

Ellie spoke softly but with a firmness Livy had heard several times. "John, the day you walked into my life was a blessing that surrounds me every moment I'm with you. I was a single mother on her own with nothing but determination to find a way to keep my family here at Sanderling Cove. You helped me as a friend and became the man who taught me what true love was by showing me tenderness and devotion, by loving my children, by making my life easier with your hard work. We were meant to be together, you and I, and I will love and support you the rest of my days. You are my everything, my reason for being."

As her grandparents kissed, Livy dabbed at her eyes with a tissue and noticed she wasn't the only one. This couple who'd been together for so many years had proved their love over and over again. She glanced at Austin feeling that same kind of bond Gran and John had demonstrated. When he smiled at her it was as if he has spoken a vow of his own.

CHAPTER FORTY-SEVEN

ELLIE

At the reception inside the dining room, Ellie stood with her girlfriends watching her daughters interact. It was a gift to see them together laughing and enjoying one another in a way they'd seldom done as young girls. Observing other members of her family and those in her cove family, she knew she'd always remember this moment, this magical day.

Liz beamed at her. "Seems to me like the five of us women have accomplished what we wanted to do. All those lovebirds out there."

"It's been a fabulous summer," said Sarah.

"We set out to make it possible to have more great grandbabies," said Ellie. "The rest is up to them."

"I'm pretty sure Adam is going to present me with another great-grand," said Karen. "Looks like Madison and her daughter, Sari, are going to become part of the family."

"Delightful news," said Pat. "Morgan told me she's not going to wait to start her family after marriage."

"How's Melissa doing?" Ellie asked. Morgan's sister, Melissa, had come to the cove for a short time and then left.

"Much better," said Pat. "She seems to have settled down, is sober, and is dating a young man who owns a cattle ranch. A small one, Melissa told me. But she sounded happy."

The women chuckled. They knew appearance was important to Melissa or had been. She was sounding different already.

"How are wedding plans coming along?" Liz asked.

"Better than I thought," said Ellie. "My daughters are finally understanding the magic of the cove and the Inn as a place for weddings. I'm pretty sure we're going to host a few family ones here in the near future."

"That makes me very happy," said Liz.

"Me, too," said Ellie. "After all, we're one big family and it only seems right."

"Amen," said Mimi.

"What are you women up to next?" John said, coming to join them. "With Ellie having more time on her hands to get into trouble, I'm sure it'll be something."

"Us? Trouble?" said Liz. "More like making sure things get done around here."

Ellie laughed with the others. One thing she knew for certain, Sanderling Cove would continue to be a hotbed of ideas for the future.

# # #

Thank you for reading *Salty Kisses*. If you enjoyed this book, please help other readers discover it by leaving a review on Amazon, Goodreads, BookBub, or your favorite site. It's such a nice thing to do.

And be sure to check out the other books in The Sanderling Cove Inn Series:

Waves of Hope
Sandy Wishes

To stay in touch and to keep up with the latest news, here's a link to sign up for my periodic newsletter!

http://bit.ly/2OQsb7s

Enjoy an excerpt from my book, *Sandy Wishes*, Book 2 in The Sanderling Cove Inn Series, which will be released in 2023:

PROLOGUE

Eleanor "Ellie" Weatherby, now Ellie Rizzo, sat on the patio of the small inn in Provence, France, thinking about her latest message from her friend and co-conspirator, Liz Ensley. Liz and the other three women who lived in Sanderling Cove on the Gulf Coast of Florida, grandmothers all, had decided to make it a special summer for their beloved grandbabies by bringing them all together. With only three great-grands in the bunch, it was time for action, and who better for their grandchildren to marry than other cove kids?

They were trying to be discreet about their matchmaking, of course, but the grandmothers all had reasons to ask their grandchildren to spend time at the cove. For Ellie, it was truly important. She'd married her long-time business partner and lover after years of living and working together so that each could provide guidance on health decisions going forward. In her seventies, Ellie had decided it was time to choose between selling the Sanderling Cove Inn or finding someone in the family willing to keep it going.

Her granddaughters—Charlotte, Brooke, and Olivia—were a marvelous trio of smart, capable young women. Her hope was that somehow one or the three of them together would be willing to keep the Inn in the family. After spending the summer managing the Inn while she and John enjoyed a long-awaited auto trip and honeymoon through Europe, the three young women should be able to give her an answer.

As for the other business at hand, Charlie had already found the love of her life in Liz's grandson, Shane. She wished them all the loving luck in the world. Brooke and Livy? More time would tell if they'd be as lucky.

CHAPTER ONE

BROOKE

Brooke Weatherby sat on the beach in the early morning light in a complete funk. She was tired of being the dependable one, the boring one out of everyone at Sanderling Cove. She'd agreed to come to the cove unaware her two cousins, Charlotte "Charlie" Bradford and Olivia "Livy" Winters, would be there. All three had been invited to help Gran and John with The Sanderling Cove Inn over the summer while Gran and John went on a long road trip in Europe. She loved her cousins and was happy to have the summer with them. But being with them sometimes made her own failing all too apparent.

She wiggled her toes in the sand, wishing she was different, that she'd find the freedom she needed to be herself. She was filled with determination. They might seem like only sandy wishes to others, but she was going to make them come true.

Gran had especially wanted Brooke to be able to spend the time away from her mother. Though sweet, her mother, Jo Weatherby, suffered from fibromyalgia and depression and depended on Brooke to be her caretaker at times and her friend at other times. It was an exhausting situation that had cost Brooke a relationship in the past. She didn't want that to happen again.

"Time to kick up your heels and have fun," Gran had told her. "You deserve it." She'd gone on to say that the co-dependent relationship with her mother wasn't healthy for either of them.

Later, leaving their small town in upstate New York and

arriving in Florida had felt to Brooke as if she'd been given wings. But it would take more than a stay on the Gulf Coast of Florida to change things permanently. Brooke had to decide just who she wanted to become away from the past. She wanted to add some much-needed freedom to her life.

Brooke studied the waves washing into shore for a quick kiss before pulling away again. The ageless pattern was soothing to her. Sandpipers and sanderlings hurry past on tiny feet, leaving their marks behind in the sand. That was one thing she wanted for herself—to leave her mark behind. Something stronger than that of caring for a sick mother.

She looked up as Livy joined her and sat on the sand beside her.

"What are you doing up this early?" Livy asked. "You're not on duty today."

On the short side with curly, strawberry-blond hair and blue eyes full of mischief, Livy was everyone's favorite. The fact that she was a fabulous baker was another reason some of the men in the cove gravitated toward her. That, and the fact that Livy was always up for a fun-filled adventure. But she was a hard worker too. She handled the kitchen duties for breakfast, along with Billy Bob, an ex-con who'd worked alongside John for years.

"I was restless and needed some time by the water to collect my thoughts," said Brooke.

Livy frowned, concern etching her brow. "Is everything all right?"

"I guess." Brooke shrugged. "I'm contemplating the future and trying to decide what I want out of life. A lot of deep thinking for sure." She brightened. "On a different, more edgy note, I'm thinking of getting a tattoo. Something to prove that I'm not still caught in a rut."

"A tattoo?" A smile spread across Livy's face. "You know

what? You, Charlie, and I should each get one. Something to always remember this summer. What design would you choose?"

"I'm not sure. What about you? A cupcake? Or cookies?"

Livy laughed. "I like the idea of a small cupcake. You could choose something like a seashell because you and Skye spend so much time looking for them."

Brooke cheered up. She and Adam Atkins' four-year-old daughter Skye had become shell-seeking buddies. Adam was a wonderful, single father who intrigued her, but they were simply friends. If Skye wasn't adorable and hadn't attached herself to Brooke, Brooke might not spend much time with them. But when Skye ran to her for a hug, Brooke would never turn her away.

Livy checked her watch and rose. "I'd better get to the kitchen. It's a slow morning, but I can't let Billy Bob think I'm not serious about my job." With Gran and John gone for the summer, Livy's task was to oversee the kitchen staff for the breakfasts for which the Inn was well known.

Billy Bob was a giant of a man, an ex-con who was frightening until you got to know him. The scowls on his face softened only slightly around other people. Tic Tacs seemed to be the only things that made him happy enough to smile. That, or one of Livy's chocolate chip cookies.

After a while, Brooke decided to go to the Inn herself. She wanted to work on the upgrade to the guest registration program Austin Ensley had set up for them. All information from there flowed to their financial reports. She'd been observing the process for a while, and she wanted to make some changes to the new system. Having worked for years in an accounting office, Brooke's role was to help with the financials for the Inn alongside Jake McDonnell, the Inn's accountant and financial advisor.

She and Jake had hit it off from the beginning. A self-made man who'd been raised by a friend of Gran's after his mother died of an overdose, Jake was a kind, ambitious, handsome man who'd never forgotten his roots. Brooke admired him for more than his looks.

When she entered the Inn, Charlotte was in the dining room chatting with a couple who'd risen early and were getting their own coffee from the sideboard in the dining room before breakfast was served. Tall and slim, with auburn hair tied back in a low ponytail, Charlotte was a striking young woman. She, like Livy and Brooke, was in her late twenties. Recently, Charlotte had become engaged to Shane Ensley. Their relationship had bloomed early and grown quickly into a deep love. Everyone in the cove, including her, thought they were perfect together.

Charlotte greeted her with a wave and walked over to her. "What's this about tattoos? Livy says we're all getting one together and mine has to be of a mermaid."

"Mermaid? That's perfect for you," said Brooke. "Yes, let's do it. I'll do some research and set something up."

Charlotte grinned. "Okay, but mine is going to be small. Nothing that could show in a wedding dress."

"That's cool. Mine will be small too, but I don't care. It's something different. I'm in such a rut." She emitted a long sigh.

Charlotte's expression grew serious. "Are you all right?"

Brooke nodded. "Just full of wishes, I guess."

"Anything I can help you with?" Charlie asked.

"No, but thanks. It's something I have to decide for myself." Feeling better, Brooke headed to the office with a cup of coffee. There, numbers were easy to work with. They were either right or wrong.

###

Brooke was still working on numbers sometime later when her cell rang. She checked caller ID. *Jo Weatherby*.

"Hi, Mom," said Brooke. She hadn't talked to her mother in days, and though they'd agreed to limit their conversations this summer, Brooke was uncertain about her mother's response, hoping she wouldn't be sent on a guilt trip.

"Hi, Brooke. It's been so long since we've talked that I had to call. How are things going with the Inn? Are you bored to tears?"

"Bored? Anything but," she quickly replied. "Gran and John have done an amazing job of managing the Inn. Charlie, Livy, and I are all busy trying to do the same plus make some improvements."

"I keep thinking of you in that hot, humid summer climate," said Jo.

Brooke knew what her mother was doing—making it sound as if she was concerned for Brooke when actually it was a lead-in to asking her when she was coming home.

Sure enough, Jo said, "I can't wait for you to come home. The house is empty without you."

"Mom, you know I'm committed for the summer and, perhaps, beyond. Nothing is going to make me change my mind." Brooke took a deep breath. "How are you feeling?"

"I've been better, but nothing for you to worry about," her mother said. "If it gets any worse, I'll call the nursing service and have them send someone to stay with me."

Guilt, like a prickly porcupine, poked Brooke in all her sensitive places. She shook her head. She couldn't go back to past behavior, rush home to help. "I'm sure they have capable people on their staff. We've used that nursing service once before. Remember?"

"Yes. They were good. Not as great as having you here, but acceptable."

“That’s how we’ll leave it, then. Sorry but I’m in the middle of working on financials here and I’d better go. Jake is due to arrive soon, and I want my work done before he gets here.”

“Okay. Love you, sweetie. Talk to you later.” Her mother clicked off the call, and Brooke let out a huge sigh. She and her mother had always been a twosome which made her fight for independence more difficult. Her father had died in Iraq before Brooke was born, leaving Jo to fend for herself. Rather than move closer to her family, Jo had opted to stay in the house in New York she and her fiancé had purchased together.

Brooke went back to her work, but her emotions were still churning. When Jake arrived, she was happy to see him. She had a few ideas she wanted to share.

After agreeing to the changes Brooke wanted to make to the registration process, Jake left the Inn. Brooke paced the office, her mind going over the conversation she’d had with her mother. She desperately wanted to do something to prove her independence. The tattoos would have to wait. She needed to do something now.

She drove to a hair salon nearby. She was tired of being the same person day after day, the one everyone depended on, the one who couldn’t seem to relax and just enjoy life.

She entered the salon, and when the owner offered a few surprising suggestions, Brooke smiled. This was more like it.

Later, purple streaks accented her brown highlighted hair. Brooke studied her image with surprise, staring at the way the purple in her hair made her hazel eyes change hues to something browner. She knew that for some people, doing something like this was no big deal. But for her, it was a daring move. She’d been programmed always to do the right, the ladylike thing.

She left for Gran's house proud of her new bold statement.

In her bedroom, she studied her reflection in the mirror still surprised by what she'd done. Of medium height, her features were a cross between Livy's and Charlie's, both cute and classic.

Livy peered into Brooke's room. "Wow, a new 'do. I love it! Wait until Charlie sees it. She'll be as surprised as I am," said Livy. "Are we meeting downstairs like always?"

"Yes." Brooke held up the papers she'd prepared for the meeting. "I've got a few new ideas for the registration of guests. That, and a quick review of where we stand on our budget."

"Great," said Livy. "I want to talk about something too."

Brooke liked that her cousins were as sincere as she about doing an outstanding job for Gran and John. She, probably more than they, enjoyed managing the Inn enough to consider doing it in the future. It was a fascinating business.

She and Livy went downstairs to the kitchen.

When Charlotte entered the room for their meeting, she took one look at Brooke and squealed. "What did you do to your hair? Turn around. Let me get a better look."

Brooke twirled in a circle.

"I love it," said Charlotte. "With my auburn hair, it wouldn't work. But on you, it looks great."

Letting out the breath she didn't realize she'd been holding, Brooke felt more confident. Charlotte was more reserved than Livy, and if she liked Brooke's attempt to be different, it was an important sign.

Livy took fresh lemonade from the refrigerator and poured them each a glass before she took a seat at the kitchen table.

"What new things do we have to discuss?" asked Brooke. As the financial manager for the Inn for the summer, she'd been designated to oversee the renovation budget.

"I've done some mockups of brochures I need to show you and Livy for approval," said Charlotte.

"I'd like to get a new grill for the kitchen," said Livy.

"Okay, let's take a look at the budget," said Brooke. "We've completed almost everything on the list of updates. The PR budget is still pretty open. The funds for the kitchen are mostly spent. Livy, how much would the grill cost? And why do we need it?"

Sitting back, listening to Livy, Brooke liked being in charge. She knew she was a capable accountant, but at her job in New York, her work had never been given the respect it deserved. She'd hoped for a partnership one day, but now the thought was unappealing. Another reason not to go back to her old job, her old life.

Charlotte agreed that Livy could have some of her PR funds for the new grill. And when she showed them the new brochures and pamphlets she wanted to have printed, Brooke and Livy eagerly gave their approval for Charlotte to take them to a printer to be produced.

Satisfied things were running smoothly, Brooke ended the meeting.

Charlotte and Livy each had plans for the evening, so Brooke decided to take a walk on the beach. The salt air, the rhythmic sound of the waves rushing to shore and retreating, and the antics of shorebirds skittering along the sand always lifted her spirits.

As she crossed the lawn and entered the sandy beach a small figure raced toward her crying, "Brooke! Brooke!"

Brooke's lips curved. She held out her arms, and Skye rushed into them. An adorable four-year-old with blond curly hair and blue eyes that missed nothing, Adam's daughter and Brooke shared a special relationship.

Skye's arms loosened around Brooke's neck. She stared at

Brooke, and then a huge smile spread across her face. "You've got purple in your hair. How did you do that? I want purple too." She patted Brooke's head gingerly, her face alight with excitement.

Brooke laughed. "I love your hair just the way it is. Like Livy's."

"But I want ..."

Before a real whining session could occur, Brooke said, "Did you find any new shells today with Mimi?"

Skye wiggled to get down and ran over to a bucket nearby, picked it up, and carried it back to her. "We found a scallop shell this morning."

Impressed, Brooke said, "You're learning the names of the shells. That's good."

"Mimi is showing me. She has a book," said Skye proudly.

Skye's great-grandmother, Mimi, walked over to them. She glanced at Brooke's hair and grinned. "Time for something new, huh?"

Brooke returned her smile. Mimi was a lovely woman, upbeat, social, easy to talk to. "Yes. I thought it was time I did something totally different for me."

"Well, I like it," said Mimi. "How are things going with your mother? Is she getting used to having you gone?"

"It's a work in progress. I talked to her earlier. She has her ups and downs."

"Ellie was especially anxious for you to spend the summer here, hoping it would change the situation for you both. I know you're working hard at the Inn, but have fun too, hear."

Brooke grinned. "That's exactly what I intend to do."

Dylan Hendrix, Adam's cousin, walked toward them. "Hey, what's up?" He stopped when he noticed Brooke's hair. "Purple?"

She grinned. "Yes."

"I like it. A shade of amethyst."

She laughed. Only Dylan, who was a well-known artist, would use that word.

"I'm thinking of going out tonight. Want to join me for dinner?" When Dylan smiled as he was doing now, his blue eyes lit.

"That would be great." She studied him. His brown hair was tied back in a man-bun, which accented the features of his face and matched his well-toned body. Dylan was a few years older than she, and his bold paintings had caught the eye of a number of famous people, sending their popularity and their prices into the stratosphere. Yet he was as humble a man as she'd ever met. She liked that about him.

Maybe like her hair, her future was about to change color, become brighter. She wished it would all come true.

About the Author

A ***USA Today* Best Selling Author**, Judith Keim is a hybrid author who both has a publisher and self-publishes. Ms. Keim writes heart-warming novels about women who face unexpected challenges, meet them with strength, and find love and happiness along the way. Her best-selling books are based, in part, on many of the places she's lived or visited and on the interesting people she's met, creating believable characters and realistic settings her many loyal readers love. Ms. Keim loves to hear from her readers and appreciates their enthusiasm for her stories.

Ms. Keim enjoyed her childhood and young-adult years in Elmira, New York, and now makes her home in Boise, Idaho, with her husband, Peter, and their lovable miniature Dachshund, Wally, and other members of her family.

While growing up, she was drawn to the idea of writing stories from a young age. Books were always present, being read, ready to go back to the library, or about to be discovered. All in her family shared information from the books in general conversation, giving them a wealth of knowledge and vivid imaginations.

"I hope you've enjoyed this book. If you have, please help other readers discover it by leaving a review on Amazon, BookBub, Goodreads, or the site of your choice. And please check out my other books:

The Hartwell Women Series
The Beach House Hotel Series
The Fat Fridays Group
The Salty Key Inn Series
Seashell Cottage Books
The Chandler Hill Inn Series
The Desert Sage Inn Series
Soul Sisters at Cedar Mountain Lodge
The Sanderling Cove Inn Series
The Lilac Lake Inn Series

"ALL THE BOOKS ARE NOW AVAILABLE IN AUDIO on Audible, iTunes, Findaway, Kobo and Google Play! So fun to have these characters come alive!"

Ms. Keim can be reached at **www.judithkeim.com**

And to like her author page on Facebook and keep up with the news, go to: **https://bit.ly/3acs5Qc**

To receive notices about new books, follow her on Book Bub: **http://bit.ly/2pZBDXq**

And here's a link to where you can sign up for her periodic newsletter! **http://bit.ly/2OQsb7s**

She is also on Twitter @judithkeim, LinkedIn, and Goodreads. Come say hello!

Acknowledgments

As always, I am eternally grateful to my team of editors, Peter Keim and Lynn Mapp, my book cover designer, Lou Harper, and my narrator for Audible and iTunes, Angela Dawe. They are the people who take what I've written and help turn it into the book I proudly present to you, my readers! I also wish to thank my coffee group of writers who listen and encourage me to keep on going. Thank you, Peggy Staggs, Lynn Mapp, Cate Cobb, Nikki Jean Triska, Joanne Pence, Melanie Olsen, and Megan Bryce. And to you, my fabulous readers, I thank you for your continued support and encouragement. Without you, this book would not exist. You are the wind beneath my wings.